BURT FRANKLIN: RESEARCH & SOURCE WORKS SERIES 862
Selected Essays in History, Economics & Social Science 313

DYNASTY OF THEODOSIUS

THE
DYNASTY OF THEODOSIUS

OR

Eighty Years' Struggle with the Barbarians

BY

THOMAS HODGKIN

BURT FRANKLIN
NEW YORK

Published by LENOX HILL Pub. & Dist. Co. (Burt Franklin)
235 East 44th St., New York, N.Y. 10017
Originally Published: 1889
Reprinted: 1971
Printed in the U.S.A.

S.B.N.: 8337-41780
Library of Congress Card Catalog No.: 78-162329
Burt Franklin: Research and Source Works Series 862
Selected Essays in History, Economics & Social Science 313

PREFACE.

—✦—

THIS little book owes its existence to an invitation
addressed to me by the Durham Ladies' Educational
Association to deliver to them a short course of historical lectures. Being allowed to choose my own
subject, I naturally chose that with which I was most
familiar, the epoch of the fall of the Western Empire:
but in order to prevent my very familiarity with that
period from leading me into diffuseness, I took the
precaution of writing the lectures, and thus, I believe,
was preserved from in any case over-passing the
prescribed limit of an hour and a quarter.

When my course was completed, I found that I
had described in brief outline so many of the leading
events recorded in the first two volumes of my book,
Italy and her Invaders, that it seemed worth while
to offer the result of my labours to those who might
not care to peruse the larger work. In order to give
a little more completeness to the book, I added a
lecture (the Second) on the political and social condition of the Romans and barbarians, which was not
included in the original course.

It will easily be understood that it is only by the
rejection of many minor details that it is possible to

reduce the picture of eighty eventful years within the limits of a compendium like the present. For most of these details, and for all discussion of the authorities on which the history of the period rests, I must refer to my larger work. Occasionally, however, I have touched upon some points not thoroughly discussed in *Italy and her Invaders*, and when I have done so, I have stated my authority in the notes.

TABLE OF CONTENTS.

———◆◆———

LECTURE I.

THE ROMAN EMPIRE.

	PAGE
Limits of the Empire	1–7
Its political organisation—	
The Senate	7–9
The People	9–13
The Emperor	13–17
Periods of Imperial History—	
I. The Julian and Flavian dynasties	17
II. The Antonine	18
III. The Age of Anarchy	18–20
IV. Diocletian: the Age of Restoration	21–24
Constantine the Great	25–28
Christianity and the Empire	28–32

LECTURE II.

THE ROMAN AND THE TEUTON.

	PAGE
I. The Roman—	
The Emperor	33–37
The official hierarchy	37–44
Social condition of the Empire	44–48
'Panem et Circenses'	49
The Slave	50
The Colonus	51
The Curialis	52

PAGE

II. The Teuton—

    Economic condition of the Germans   .   .   .   55–60

    German land-system   60–62

    Relation of the Village-community to the State   62–65

    The Pagus or Gau   65

    Kingship and national unity   .   .   .   67–70

    The Folc-gemot   70–71

    Election of the King   72

LECTURE III.

THE COMING OF THE HUNS.

German ethnology   73

The Goths   75

Ulfilas   77–79

Athanaric and Fritigern   79–80

Irruption of the Huns   80–83

The Visigoths seek an asylum in the Empire .   86–87

The Visigoths cross the Danube .   .   .   88

Roman Emperors: Valentinian, Valens, Gratian .   90–91

The banquet at Marcianople .   .   .   91–93

Gothic War: battle of Ad Salices .   .   .   94

Battle of Hadrianople   96–99

LECTURE IV.

THEODOSIUS.

The Goths besiege Constantinople .   .   .   101

Failures of the Goths as besiegers .   .   .   102

The massacre of the Gothic boy-hostages .   .   104

Parentage of Theodosius   106

Theodosius associated in the Empire .   .   .   107

Orthodoxy of Theodosius   108–110

Athanaric at Constantinople   111

The Goths become Foederati .   .   .   113–117

Insurrection of Antioch   117–120

Insurrection of Thessalonica .   .   .   120–122

Usurpation of Maximus   123–126

His defeat and death   127

Eugenius and Arbogast   128–130

	PAGE
Battle of the Frigidus	131
Death of Theodosius	132
His character	133

LECTURE V.

ALARIC.

	PAGE
The sons of Theodosius, Arcadius and Honorius	134
Their ministers, Rufinus and Stilicho	135–137
Alaric chosen King of the Visigoths	137
Alaric invades Greece	139
Stilicho forbidden to defend it	139
Murder of Rufinus	141–142
Second campaign of Stilicho against Alaric	143
Alaric as Roman governor of Illyricum	143
Alaric's first invasion of Italy	145–147
Invasion by Radagaisus	148–151
Revolt of Constantine in Britain	152
Negotiations between Stilicho and Alaric	153
Death of Arcadius	155
Mutiny at Ticinum. Stilicho slain	156–158
Alaric's first siege of Rome	159–161
Alaric's second siege of Rome	162
Attalus Emperor	162–164
Alaric's third siege and capture of Rome	164–166
Death of Alaric	167

LECTURE VI.

PLACIDIA : ATTILA.

	PAGE
Placidia—	
Historical perspective	170
Early life of Placidia : her captivity	171
Ataulfus, successor of Alaric	172
His marriage with Placidia	174
Death of Ataulfus	175
Second marriage, widowhood, and exile of Placidia	176
Death of Honorius	176
Rise and fall of Joannes. Valentinian III, Emperor	177
Regency of Placidia	178
Aetius	179

PAGE

Attila—

Accession of Attila : his character and appearance . 180–182

Extent of his Empire 182–184

His Embassies to Constantinople . . . 184

The vases of Sirmium 185

Honoria's ring 185

Description by Priscus of Attila's palace . . 186

    ,,   ,,   the banquet . . . 187–190

Deaths of Placidia and Theodosius II . . . 191

Marcian and Pulcheria reign 191

Attila prepares for war with the West . . 192

Alliance between the Empire and the Visigoths . . 192–193

Attila's invasion of Gaul 193

Siege of Orleans 194

Battle of Châlons (so called) 195–197

Attila's retreat 197

Attila invades Italy 198

Capture of Aquileia 198

The founders of Venice 199

Attila at Milan 200

Embassy of Pope Leo 201

Return and death of Attila 202

The Hunnish power broken 203

LECTURE VII.

Gaiseric.

Early history of the Vandals 204

The Vandals enter Gaul 205–207

They cross the Pyrenees and enter Spain . . . 207

Death of Gunderic : accession of Gaiseric . . 209

Bonifacius invites the Vandals to enter Africa . . 209–211

The Vandals transported to Africa . . . 212

Bonifacius repents and returns to Ravenna . . 215

Siege of Hippo 216

Capture of Carthage 217

Appearance, character, and career of Gaiseric . . 218–220

Vandal land-settlement 220

Law of succession to the throne . . . 221

Persecution of the Catholics 221–225

Table of Contents.

	PAGE
Valentinian murders Aetius	226
Death of Valentinian III. Accession of Maximus . .	228
Gaiseric's Expedition to Rome. Plunder of the City .	229–232
Captivity of the widow and daughters of Valentinian .	232
Further fortunes of the Theodosian family . .	233
Conclusion	234

FAMILY OF VALENTINIAN.

[Emperors of the East are printed in *Italic* capitals.]

GRATIAN,
of Cibalis in Pannonia.

VALENTINIAN I, born 321, proclaimed Emperor 364, died 375.

VALENS, born about 329, Emperor 364, slain at the battle of Hadrianople 378.

VALENS, surnamed Galata, born 366, died 371.

SEVERA, or Marina (divorced).

JUSTINA, widow of the usurper Magnentius (he was slain 353).

A daughter of Emperor Constantius II.

GRATIAN, born about 359, associated with his father as Augustus 367, slain by order of Maximus 383.

LAETA (present with her mother at the siege of Rome 408).

VALENTINIAN II, born about 371, Emperor 375, dethroned by Maximus 387, restored 388, slain by order of Arbogast 392.

JUSTA.

GRATA.

GALLA, married in 387 to THEODOSIUS I, died 394.

GALLA PLACIDIA.

VALENTINIAN III, &c.

FAMILY OF THEODOSIUS.

[Emperors of the East are printed in *Italic* capitals.]

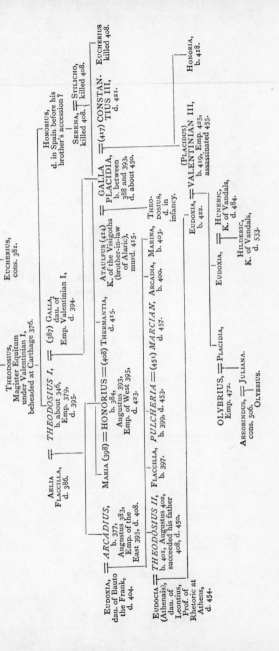

ERRATA.

Page 27, line 5 from bottom, *for* 523 *read* 323
,, 91, ,, 16, *for* get *read* yet

THE DYNASTY OF THEODOSIUS.

LECTURE I.

THE ROMAN EMPIRE.

IN Longfellow's Golden Legend the following question is asked:—

> 'Say to me
> What the great Voices Four may be
> That quite across the world do flee
> And are not heard by men?'

and this answer given:—

> 'The Voice of the Sun in heaven's dome,
> The Voice of the murmuring of Rome,
> The Voice of a Soul that goeth home,
> And the Angel of the Rain.'

'The voice of the murmuring of Rome.' That was indeed a mighty voice; how all-powerful, how nearly equivalent to the voice of the whole civilised human race, is more vividly impressed upon us by every year of deeper study of the history of the world fifteen centuries ago.

Let us try by a very rapid summary to indicate *Extent of* the meaning which the words 'Imperium Roma- *the Roman* num' conveyed to him who heard them in the days when the Temple of Jupiter Capitolinus was still standing and still thronged with earnest worshippers.

North Britain.

Let us go forth from this city which clusters on its seven hills around the Tomb of St. Cuthbert. Those hills are untrodden forest or undistinguished pasture-ground, and all the glory of architecture and all the wealth of sacred associations which will one day crown them are unknown, for we are now in the second century after Christ, and Durham is neither *castra* nor *mansio* nor *mutatio* in the map of Roman Britain. But if we go a few miles up the Wear, near to that place in 'the land of Oaks,' where the Bishop of Durham will one day build his castle, we shall find there, upon a high promontory of table-land overlooking the stream, the spacious camp of Vinovia with its baths and its hypocausts, doubtless also with its temple and its magazines. Here we strike a great Roman road. Follow that road north-wards over the hills, and you will come to the camp of Lanchester on the Browney. Another stretch over wild moorlands, and we reach Ebchester, in the pleasant valley of the Derwent. Another, and we strike the Tyne at Corstopitum (Corbridge). And so on by more camps and stations than I need weary you with the names of, till we reach the great camp, or rather series of camps, which surround the high altar-like hill of Birrenswark in Dumfriesshire, over-looking the sandy Solway. Yet still the Roman road is running northwards, till at last it reaches the Wall of Antoninus, somewhere near the Frith of Clyde.

Midland and Southern Britain.

Southwards the same road pursues its course, un-compromising and undeviating, over the great ridge of hills which separates you from the Tees. Across the Swale at Cataractonium it leads us to Isurium, which will one day be represented by the pleasant old-fashioned village of Boroughbridge, and where we see for the first time those pictured floors, the tesselated pavements which are so abundant in Southern Britain and in Gaul. Then it takes us to Eboracum, the great Roman city of the North, the home of the Sixth Legion, the place where the aged Severus will lay down the purple at the bidding of Death, and where the young Constantine will assume it at the bidding of the soldiery. Thence across the country south-westwards, over those hills and dales of Yorkshire and Lancashire, which are now among the poorest and most solitary, as they will one day be among the richest and the most thickly populated portions of the island of the Britons. So we reach Deva, or Chester on the Dee, where the Twentieth Legion have built their stately city, with its temples, its baths, and its spacious praetorium for their commanding officer. And so from thence, through Cheshire and Staffordshire, and on by a route pretty nearly coinciding with that which will, after many centuries, be taken by the North-Western Railway, till at last we reach that city, comparatively unimportant in the official map of Roman Britain, but which the concourse of merchants is even now making important in spite of prefects and procurators, 'the city formerly known as Londinium, but now named Augusta.'

In our own day, at nearly every step of our course along this great highway, which our ancestors named

Existing traces of Roman occupation. the Watling Street, there is some trace of the Roman legionary and his sojourn in our island. Here the coins of some military treasure chest buried in haste and never reclaimed; there the shells of the oysters or the bones of the beef which the soldiers consumed; here a dedication to some native god bearing an uncouth name, with whom they thought it safer to be on friendly terms; there the pathetic epitaph of a departed wife 'who lived with her husband xxx years, "*sine ulla macula*,"' with no spot upon her goodness; here the walls of a camp turned by centuries into mere grassy mounds, but still by their rectangular shape rounded at the corners, showing the handiwork of the Roman surveyor; there an inscription recording the rebuilding of a bath or a granary, '*vetustate conlapsum*' (which had fallen in through age), and reminding us how òld and venerable the buildings erected by the first conquerors of Britain must have appeared long before the last Roman soldier, standing upon the stern of the departing vessel, waved his sad '*Vale Britannia*' to our island.

Boundaries of the Roman World. All these vestiges of the great world-Empire, when one examines them patiently day after day, as it has often been my privilege to do in travelling along one of the great Roman roads in our own country or abroad, produce an effect upon the mind incomparably stronger and deeper than results from simply reading the story of the conquest of a province in the pages of Caesar or Tacitus. And now multiply this picture at least thirty-fold in order to make it justly represent the whole extent of the Empire. Cross the sea from 'Londinium, now Augusta,' to the mouth of the Rhine. Travel for days up that stately river and see the legionaries swarming upon its western, and not unknown upon its eastern bank. Trace the 300 miles of stake-covered rampart which join the Middle Rhine to the Middle Danube, and along every mile of which a Roman soldier is tramping. Descend the Danube from Ratisbon to the Euxine and see every foot of its right bank held by Rome, who for more than a century holds a province on the left bank also (the province of Dacia), and stations her legionaries on the crests of the Carpathian Mountains. Take ship and sail over the foggy Euxine, and there, in its extreme south-eastern corner, near where Jason and his companions sought the Golden Fleece, recognise once more the Roman boundary. Follow that boundary over the mountains of Armenia to the upper waters of the Tigris. Cross 'the great river, the River Euphrates,' near the place where Eliezer waited for Rebekah by the well; and then encompassing Damascus and the mysterious cities of Bashan, let the border come down past the Dead Sea, past Mount Pisgah and Mount Sinai, and so overleaping the Red Sea, let it reach the valley of the Nile. Here the frontier towards the barbarism of Ethiopia is the same that the modern protectors of Egypt have drawn close to the city of Syene (now Assouan) ; leaving 800 miles of the rich Nile valley as the granary of Rome. All along the northern coast of Africa, Cyrene, Tripolis, Carthage, Numidia, Mauretania, whatever there is of civilised, stable, wealth-producing life (and it is a broad enough belt in some places) is all Roman by obedience, and much of it Latin by speech. At last the boundary goes out at the Atlantic Ocean where Hercules once relieved Atlas of his load. Men gazing forth upon the waste of waters, and half discovering, half dreaming, concerning the Fortunate Isles beyond, are constrained at length to admit the fact that the great Empire has found its limit, and that if there be other worlds to the West they are worlds beyond the world of Rome.

The Orbis Romanus nearly coincided with the Orbis Terrarum. It was an immense extent of territory which the Roman god Terminus thus marked out, and (as has been often pointed out, but is a fact of the greatest importance) it more nearly embraced the whole of the then known and civilised world than any Empire that has since been seen. True, the mysterious river of Asiatic civilisation, as represented by China and India, flowed on, not blending its waters with those which the Tiber ruled. But these countries were practically altogether beyond the horizon of the Empire. During the first three centuries of our era there was only one civilised power of which Rome was conscious as a possible rival to herself, and that was the power of Persia. Her sovereign, whether he were known as Parthian or Persian, as Arsacid or Sassanid, took to himself proud titles, calling himself 'King of Kings,' and so forth, and often by his devastating raids inflicted sore disaster on the Eastern provinces of Rome; but the Empire was certainly far the stronger power, and many of the abler Emperors could probably, if they had deemed it wise to make the attempt, have accomplished what Julian so narrowly missed and what Heraclius triumphantly performed, the overthrow of the Persian monarchy.

This vast territory had been acquired by the municipality of an Italian city under a government which was in some respects the best adapted for gaining and for consolidating dominion that the world has ever seen. S. P. Q. R.: these four letters formed the talisman which floated on the victorious standards of Rome, whether they crowned the misty heights of the Cheviots or were mirrored in the waters of the Orontes. The Senate and the People of Rome: we must pause for a few moments on these words to consider what they implied. *Government of the Roman State.*

Senatus Populus Que Romanus.

(1) The Senate of Rome, in its best days reminding the beholder of an assembly of Kings, debating the affairs of the Republic with a gravity, an earnestness and a conciseness very unlike the showy rhetoric of a Greek *Ecclesia* or the vapid verbiage of a modern House of Commons or House of Representatives: this was the body which gave coherence and unity to the policy of the great Latin city, which prevented it from being swayed to and fro by such gusts of passion or misplaced sentiment as ruined the Empire of Athens; which caused it to pursue, century after century, the same undeviating course, and to act *The Roman Senate under the Republic.*

upon the same maxims of statesmanship—hard maxims often, and inspired by a terrible egotism, but successful. It was the Senate which enabled the Roman State to feel the proud confidence that was expressed with less justice by that patient toiler, Philip of Spain, 'Time and I against any one else in the world.'

Not a mere hereditary aristocracy. One source of the Senate's strength was derived from the fact that it was never in theory and seldom in practice a mere hereditary aristocracy. Election to some one of the great offices of the State into which the kingly power had been divided, Consulship, Praetorship, Quaestorship, was the door by which entrance was gained into the 'assembly of Kings'— and this election in the better days of the Republic implied a certain amount of popular respect if not of popular favour—but once admitted, the Senator had his seat practically for life, and needed not to tremble at every changing wind of popular opinion, lest the withdrawal of the favour of his constituents should doom him to political annihilation. The chasm which once separated the Patrician from the Plebeian, and which made it impossible for the latter to enter the Senate, had been filled up long before Rome began to play her great part among the nations of the earth: but it is true that a new aristocracy of consular families, partly Patrician and partly Plebeian, had arisen on the ruins of the old. A Terentius Varro, a Marius, a Cicero could by great energy, by military successes, or by surpassing eloquence, break through into the charmed circle, but the outcry that was raised at the presumption of such a *novus homo* showed that the event was a rare one.

One institution, however, which modern aristo- *The Cen-* cracies would do well to copy, tended to save the *sorship.* Senate from the worst perils of a hereditary oligarchy. To be ruled by a proud nobility which respects itself is perhaps not pleasant, but it is endurable. But to be ruled by 'hereditary legislators' who do not observe the ordinary decencies of life is an ignominy too galling to be borne. The power of the *Censor* to degrade from his Senatorial office any man who offended against the strict old-fashioned code of Roman morality, a power which in the best days of the Republic was wielded with merciless severity and without respect of persons, must have largely contributed to that moral ascendency of the Senate which made it for four centuries as supreme in Roman politics as the House of Commons has been for the last two centuries in the politics of Britain.

(2) The People of Rome, the Quirites, assembled *The People* by their centuries or their tribes, under an Italian *of Rome.* sky, in the Campus Martius or the Forum— these also had their allotted share in the develop- ment of the greatness of Rome : these formed the strong steadily beating heart, without which all the accumulated wisdom of the Senate, the brain of the State, would have been of no avail. Questions of peace and war, and questions of poli- tical reform, were brought before them, generally, it

is true, on the motion of the Senate, but so as to cast the final responsibility on the people ; and during the greater part of the lifetime of the Republic those solemn trials of political offenders which correspond most nearly to our own impeachments took place at the bar of the popular assembly.

The Tribunes. To guard these rights and to secure the meanest citizen of Rome from oppression on the part of some haughty aristocrat, the Tribunes of the Commonalty were called into being, that unique class of magistrates whose power of 'intercession' could bring the whole machinery of the State to a deadlock, and upon whose 'sacro-sanct' persons the proudest Consul, fresh from victory over the enemies of Rome, might not lay hands without incurring the penalty of outlawry. The office which the Member of Parliament has hitherto discharged when he brings the grievance of a constituent before the House of Commons ; the office of redresser of all wrongs and browbeater of all magistrates, which the Public Press has of later time arrogated to itself— these offices were for centuries discharged by the Tribunes of the Commonalty. Upon the whole we may believe that the Tribunician power was a useful counterpoise to the immense authority vested in Consuls and Praetors : but it was always a power which in the hands of a dishonest demagogue might be abused for the purpose of obstruction. It was always useful only as a brake is useful to the driver of a railway train ; and in the latter days of the Republic it was a brake suddenly and clumsily applied, by which the Engine of the State was being continually thrown off the line.

But, such as they were, these two great deposi- *Political* taries of power, the Senate and the People, wrought *decline.* together in reasonable harmony, and upon the whole for the good of Rome and the fast widening Roman world, during the two centuries which inter- *B.C.* 367– vened between the admission of Plebeians to the 146. Consulate and the Third Punic War. With the fall of Rome's old rival, Carthage, a rapid change for the worse manifested itself in the Roman character. Corruption entered the Senate and brutal violence disgraced the Assembly of the People. The young Roman politician half ruined himself over the shows of gladiators and wild beasts that were to purchase from the commonalty his election to the successive offices which were the steps in the ladder of his promotion. The mob cheered and laughed, but the provinces groaned, for out of their plundered cities and beggared agriculture the Propraetor or Proconsul reckoned to recoup himself for the heavy entrance-fees which he had paid to gain admission to the Roman Senate. These abuses became at length too glaring for even the seared consciences of Roman politicians to endure. Laws against official extortion, '*de repetundis pecuniis*,' were passed by the people—a doubtful boon to the provincials, for now the governor robbed them, not for himself only, but for the rivals and the demagogues whose silence he had to purchase by bribes. In the train of the governor went the usurer, lending money at ruinous rates to the provincial to enable him to pay the clamorous tax-gatherer. Even Brutus, that Puritan among Roman statesmen, sought to compel the inhabitants of Salamis to pay him compound interest at the rate of 48 per cent. per annum. Under these accumulated oppressions the fair countries round the Mediterranean were fast sinking into misery and despair, the very life-blood being drained out of them by the insatiable oligarchs of Rome. And during the greater part of this time, while the Senators were treating the civilised world as their own private farm, and farming it like a tenant who is under notice to quit and will get all he can out of the soil, the so-called People of Rome were every year sinking lower and lower into degradation, becoming a mere mob of freedmen and foreigners, the collected sewage of the world. The Constitution—notwithstanding a temporary reaction under Sulla—was becoming more and more democratic, as the people were becoming more utterly unworthy to be trusted with power. Armed bands of hired bravoes fought with one another in the streets of Rome, and on the day of a hotly-disputed election or the passing of an unpopular law, the statues in the Forum were splashed with the blood of the slain.

Shelley on the decay of Roman freedom. I know no words which more vividly bring before our minds the contrast between the Rome of Cincinnatus and the Rome of Clodius than this verse from Shelley's ' Ode to Liberty ' :—

'Then Rome was, and from thy deep bosom, fairest
Like a wolf-cub, from some Cadmean Maenad
  She drew the milk of greatness, though thy dearest[1]
From that Elysian food was yet unweanéd.
  And many a deed of terrible uprightness
By thy sweet love was sanctified,
        And in thy smile and by thy side
        Saintly Camillus lived and firm Atilius[2] died.
But when blood stained thy robe of vestal whiteness,
  And gold profaned thy Capitolian throne,
Thou didst desert with spirit-winged lightness
  The Senate of the oppressors : they sank prone
Slaves of one tyrant : Palatinus sighed
        Faint echoes of Ionian song. That tone
        Thou didst delay to hear, lamenting to disown.'

'Slaves of one tyrant.' That was the doom, the righteous doom of the Roman Senate and People. Corruption above and anarchy below had slain that Public Virtue without which a Republic cannot live : and now the only hope of the world lay in the up-rising of some one man who should save Rome from herself, and rescue from her Senate and People the provinces which they had won but could no longer govern.

This necessary work was performed by the man *Caesar.* who stands head and shoulders above all other statesmen, as Isaiah above all other Prophets, as Shakespeare above all other Dramatists,—the man whose name still means Emperor to more than a hundred millions of mankind, GAIUS JULIUS CAESAR. It may be truly said that the further we get away from Caesar the Dictator, the greater his work appears. Superficial students of history used to think

---

[1] Greece.   [2] Regulus.

of it as only lasting for five centuries (yet five centuries, the interval of time that separates us from Chaucer and Wycliffe, is not a contemptible interval in a nation's life): but the more scientific school of modern historians rightly claim that the work of Julius Caesar, the organisation of *Imperium Romanum*, outlived not only the fall of Rome, but the fall of Constantinople also, and was only destroyed by 'the bastard Caesar,' Napoleon, in 1806, if indeed it be not, in a sense, living still.

Theory of the Principate.
As the various offices of the Republic had been formed chiefly out of the power of the ancient kings, it might have seemed the obvious course to recombine them into one, and crown Caesar king. Warned by the murmurs of the crowd on the day of the Lupercalia, but also doubtless following his own instinct as a statesman, Julius—and his nephew Augustus after him—chose a wiser course. The name of Republic should still remain : S.P.Q.R. should still be inscribed on the banners of the legions, but the powers of the Republic should all be grasped in a single hand. There had been Dictators created for special emergencies : Julius would be a life-long Dictator. Successful generals had been saluted Imperator by their soldiers on the field of battle : Julius would be emphatically *the* Imperator. Grave and reverend men, the fathers of the Senate, had been hailed with the title *Princeps* : Augustus would now in middle life be greeted as Princeps. Above all, the Tribunes of the Commonalty had possessed enormous powers for the prevention of

legislation of which they disapproved, and their persons had been invested with especial sanctity. Augustus would now gather into himself all the obstructive powers of the whole College of Tribunes, and his person should be 'sacro-sanct' as theirs had been. Special defenders of the Commonalty were now no longer needed. The new Imperator claimed, and not altogether without reason, that *he* was defender of the people, and therefore each year by a fresh and solemn act he was 'invested with the Tribunician power.'

Our own Constitutional monarchy is often called *A Monar-* 'a Republic veiled under monarchical forms.' The *chy under Republican* Empire of the Caesars was just the reverse: an *forms.* absolute monarchy veiled under the forms of a Republic. The analogy may be carried a little further. Just as every really great and patriotic Prime Minister, under a Constitutional monarchy *Deference* like ours, veils somewhat of the power which in *of the good Emperors* fact is his under the forms of deference to the *to the* throne, and does this not in servile adoration for *Senate.* rank, but because he knows that in the institution of Monarchy there is a fund of latent power which it were unwise to squander, and which may one day be sorely needed for the defence of the life of the nation against enemies from without or from within, even so the greatest and best of the Roman Emperors, while holding all power in their hands, used that power as much as possible in harmony with the Senate and in conformity with the Senate's advice; and thus, while preserving the prestige of an ancient

and venerable assembly, also retained in the State a
force which might operate as a counterpoise, though
a feeble one, should the vast powers of the Emperor
pass into the keeping of a foolish or wicked successor. But while the good and patriotic Emperors

*The bad
Emperors
delighted
in degrad-
ing it.*

—Augustus, Trajan, Marcus Aurelius, Claudius
Gothicus, Probus—delighted to magnify the moral
authority of the Senate, the weak and dissolute
Emperors, maddened by the possession of absolute
power, delighted to trample upon and insult it.
Caligula forced Senators of the highest rank to
walk for miles before his chariot, or to wait upon
him at table, each clad in the linen girdle of a slave.
Nero wrung from the loathing Senate a formal ap-
probation of the murder of his mother, and insisted
on 400 of its members performing as gladiators in
the Amphitheatre. And Domitian, according to the
well-known story in the pages of Juvenal, summoned
the trembling Conscript Fathers in the dead of
night to deliberate on the best manner of cooking
an enormous turbot.

*The Pro-
vinces were
the gainers
by the
Imperial
system.*

But though the Senators groaned under the insults and the cruelty of the bad Emperors (of whom
in the first century of the Empire there was undoubtedly a terrible preponderance over the good
ones) there can be little doubt that for the Empire at
large the change to the Imperial system was an
enormous benefit. The populace of Rome had
their rations and their gladiatorial exhibitions (*panem et circenses*) regularly, and what was more important, the police and the water supply of the

great City were attended to as they had never been before. The provinces were no longer exposed to the unchecked cupidity of some dissolute aristocrat, eager to suck them dry during his short term of office and then to hurry back to play the great game of politics in Rome. Unjust governors, men like Pontius Pilate and Felix, undoubtedly still bore sway ; but at least they had as a rule a longer term of office, and less need therefore to drain the province all at once. And the thought of the terrible Caesar at Rome, who, however cruel and rapacious himself, was generally quick to punish cruelty and rapacity in others, the dread of hearing, after a manifestly unjust sentence, the fateful words pronounced, 'Provoco ad Caesarem[1],' kept many a provincial governor, who may have been at heart no better than Verres or Gabinius, from shearing the helpless sheep before him as closely as they would have been shorn in the later days of the Republic. It is one of the commonplaces of history that even Nero himself was hated only in Rome, and that after his death the story that he still lived and would one day return and resume the purple, was told and lovingly cherished in many of the provinces.

The history of the Empire naturally groups itself into periods, each of about a century in duration. The Julian dynasty, from the battle of Actium (B.C. 31) to the death of Nero (A. D. 68), fills up ninety-nine years. We pass lightly over the twenty-seven

Chief periods of Imperial history. I. The Julian Dynasty, 99 years.

---

[1] 'I appeal unto Caesar.'

(*B.C.* 31–
A.D. 68.)
*The Fla-
vian Dy-
nasty*, 27
years.
(69–96.)
*II. The
Antonines,
84 years.*
(96–180.)
years of the Flavian dynasty (69–96), which is in
some respects like a copy of the Julian, Vespasian
being a somewhat commonplace Augustus and
Domitian a vulgar Nero, and we come to the great
and glorious age of the Antonines[1]. For eighty-
four years (A. D. 96–180) a series of sovereigns, the
best, the wisest and the most statesmanlike that the
world has ever seen—Nerva, Trajan, Hadrian,
Antoninus, Marcus—sat upon the throne of the
world. What has been already said as to the
happiness of the provinces under the Julian
dynasty might be said without any qualification,
as far as the rulers could bring happiness, of the
century of Antonine rule. But according to the
trite quotation—

> ' How small, of all that human hearts endure,
>   That part which laws or kings can cause or cure.'

The course of nature seems as if it had been out
of joint during that otherwise happy century. Destructive earthquakes, wide-wandering pestilences
and grievous famines marked its course ; and at
the close of it came that terrible irruption of barbarians from the lands of the Middle Danube which
is known as the Marcomannic War, and which
very nearly brought about the fall of the Roman
Empire two centuries too soon.

*III. The
Age of
Anarchy,*
105 *years.*
(180–285.)
The stately and philosophic virtue of the Antonine Emperors led to a terrible anti-climax—
the mad sensuality and cruelty of the bull-necked

---

[1] Strictly speaking the Ulpii, Aelii, Antonini, and Annii. But
Antoninus is the best central name for the dynasty.

Commodus. And now began that terrible third century, in which the great World-Empire seemed perpetually as if it were on the point of going to pieces, through its own weakness and corruption, before the barbarians were ready even to gather up its fragments. It had been discovered 'that an emperor could be made elsewhere than in Rome,' and in every province, almost in every legionary camp, there was an upstart General eager to avail himself of this discovery, eager to wrap himself in the purple and to lay hold of what the Greek historians call ἡ τῶν ὅλων ἀρχή, 'the rule of the universe.' The strongest memory can hardly retain the names of all the obscure adventurers who thus blossomed into a little temporary notoriety, and who were murdered by a rival or fell on the field of battle before their purple had lost the lustre of its newness. Province thus fighting against province and civil war being the normal condition of the Empire, the misery and poverty which everywhere prevailed can hardly be imagined, and are but scantily pourtrayed for us by the wretched historians of the time. Two things, however, always occur to my mind as typical of this woeful age—its coinage and its camps. Take a *Debased* coin of one of the earlier Emperors, say a bronze *Coinage.* sestertius of Domitian, which lies before me while I write: see the clear bold relief of the laurel-crowned head, the sharp, well-cut letters of the inscription, and then compare it with a (so-called) silver denarius of Valerian or Gallienus—a thin bit of copper with a wash of silver or pewter over it, and upon it the barbarous effigy of a head wearing a radiated crown and surrounded by an almost illegible inscription. From a mere glance at the coins you feel at once that the owner of a sestertius (whose nominal value was twopence-halfpenny) under Domitian was a richer man than the owner of a denarius (the equivalent of four sestertii) under Gallienus.

Degenerate Architecture. And the camps: go to Housesteads or Chesters and see the splendid blocks of masonry which belong to the age of the Antonines; see the masonry of a very different and far inferior kind, small and mean and easily overthrown, which marks the age of Constantine, after the close of the third century. But in between these two periods of original building and late repair you may often find a mass of confused *débris*, sometimes with the marks of fire upon them. That shapeless mound tells the story of the third century. While every little Tribune or Centurion was coquetting with the soldiers under his command, relaxing discipline and permitting plunder, in the hope that they might some morning rush to the Praetorium, put on him the purple robe and hail him as Imperator, meantime the *Pax Romana* was becoming a bitter bye-word over all the Empire, and in our own country the savage Caledonians were breaking down the barrier of Hadrian, setting fire to Cilurnum and Borcovicus, swarming across the Tyne and Tees, and carrying fire and sword far into the heart of Britain.

The deliverer of the world from this tempest of *IV. The* anarchy and disruption, the true Second Founder *Age of Re-storation.,* of the Empire was the son of a Dalmatian slave, *93 years,* Diocletian. As his reign began A.D. 285, as the work *(285–378.)* of reorganisation which was commenced by him was continued by Constantine (306–337), and as the political system thus inaugurated lasted unimpaired till 378, the date of the battle of Hadrianople, we may call this the fourth century of the Empire, the period of Restoration.

The great objects aimed at and accomplished by *Objects of* Diocletian were the increase of the majesty of the *the Diocle-tianic re-* Imperial office, the equable diffusion of defensive *form.* power through all parts of the Empire, the welding of a strong chain of rights and responsibilities which should vibrate from the Emperor on his throne to the lowest official in the most distant province.

(1) The increased majesty of the Emperor's office. *Increased* All pretence of his being only the first citizen in a *veneration for the* Republic, only the most eminent member of the *Imperial* Senate, and so on, was now done away with. The *dignity.* Emperor now wore on his head a pearl-bordered diadem, on his feet sandals studded with gems ; he was surrounded by a splendid retinue, and the peti-tioner who approached him—though he were a mem-ber of one of the proudest families in the Roman Senate—had to prostrate himself on the ground and *adore* the Imperial Majesty. Thus at length the Roman Imperator stood fully revealed, a monarch as haughty and as absolute as Darius or Sapor. In all this, censorious critics traced the overweening

pride of the Dalmatian slave's son exalted to the pinnacle of earthly greatness : yet it is probable that policy had as much share as pride in the self-exaltation of Diocletian. During the long troubles of the third century, when every legion was making and unmaking Emperors, the highest office in the State had lost all dignity and all prestige : and if it was really to recover itself and become, as Diocletian would have it, the true centre of gravity of the State, it was necessary that it should once again seem awful and majestic. The same statesmanlike spirit which dictated to Augustus the suppression of the visible signs of regal magnificence, suggested to Diocletian their multiplication and embellishment.

Division of labour. (2) It had become manifest to a statesman's eye that the vast Roman world could no longer be ruled from Rome alone. On the Rhine, on the Danube, on the Euphrates, strong armies were required to guard the frontiers : yet it was precisely from these armies, strangers to the Imperial city and to the person of the legitimate Augustus, that the brood of usurpers and tyrants, claimants for the Imperial purple, was being perpetually recruited. Diocletian now carved out the Roman Empire into four great Prefectures, each large enough to satisfy the ambition of a Charles V or a Louis XIV, and gave to each of these Prefectures its own court, its own capital, its own elaborately organised official hierarchy.

The four Prefectures. I. 'The Gauls,' comprising Britain, Gaul, Spain, and part of Morocco, and reaching from the Firth of

Clyde to Mount Atlas, had its centre of government at Augusta Trevirorum (Trier on the Moselle).

II. 'Italy,' comprising Raetia, Italy, Sicily, and the wealthy provinces of Africa, was still in theory governed from Rome; but practically its Emperor during the whole of the fourth century was generally resident at Mediolanum (Milan).

III. Illyricum, the smallest of the four Prefectures, included the provinces of the Middle Danube, the western portion of the country lately known as Turkey in Europe, and Greece. Sirmium on the Save was generally the residence of its Emperor.

IV. All the rest of the Empire formed the rich and important Prefecture of the East (Oriens). Its Emperor for the most part resided at Antioch, from whence he watched the ever menacing attitude of the Sassanid kings of Persia.

The great scheme of Imperial government matured *Transmis-* by the brain of Diocletian, provided not only for the *sion of the Imperial* exercise but also for the transmission of power. *power.* The adoptive system, which had given to the Empire all the noblest sovereigns of the Antonine period, was to be revived in all its vigour. Two Emperors ruling as Augusti were to adopt two younger colleagues as their sons, who were to bear the humbler title of Caesar, and were to administer those Prefectures in which the danger of war was the keenest, and the labour of ruling the most severe. As in the course of nature the two senior partners, the Augusti, moved off the scene, the Caesars were to take their

place and adopt two new Caesars to ease them of
their burden, and one day inherit their dignity. An
elaborate and ingenious scheme, and one which might
conceivably have preserved the Empire from civil
war at least for two or three generations, but which
in fact was broken to pieces by that longing after the
hereditary transmission of power and wealth which
is one of the deepest instincts of humanity. Diocletian and Maximian (a brave, uncultivated soldier)
were the two first Augusti : Constantius and Galerius
the two first Caesars. After a prosperous reign
of twenty years, enfeebled health and perhaps a
desire to see with his own eyes the success of his
great design, induced Diocletian voluntarily to resign
Abdication the purple, and Maximian, who had no such philoso-
of Diocle- phical inclinations and who was still in the lusty
tian, 305. vigour of middle life, was compelled to follow the
example of his patron. Thus did Constantius and
Galerius become the two new Augusti, but Galerius,
who was the son-in-law and special confidant of Diocletian, had the choice of the two new Caesars, and
chose a nephew and a dependent of his own, Maximin
Daza and Severus, neither of them really fitted for
'the rule of all things.' Constantius, a man of mild
and gentle temper, away in distant Britain and already
smitten by disease, acquiesced in the nominations of
his self-seeking partner ; but the offspring and the
soldiers of Constantius rebelled against an arrangement so one-sided and inequitable. Constantine, the
brave young son of Constantius by his concubine
Helena, now in his thirty-second year, was at Nico-

media in Bithynia when Diocletian's abdication threw
the direction of the affairs of the Imperial partnership
into the hands of Galerius, who viewed him with no
friendly eye, and would fain have kept him in honourable captivity in Asia. Repeated letters from his
colleague Constantius at length wrung from him
the required permission for the young man's departure, and Constantine, according to a well-known
story, starting on the long journey across Thrace
by the Danube and the Rhine, caused the horses at
the first few Imperial post-stations to be hamstrung,
in order to prevent any courier from overtaking him
with a revocation of the order. He reached York
in safety; he made a successful campaign in Cale-
donia under his father's auspices, and when that *Death of*
father returned to York to die, the legionaries, led *Constan-*
by a Teutonic chief Crocus, king of the Alamanni, *vation of*
who held high command among them, insisted with *Constan-*
one voice, that the diadem and the purple of the *July, 306.*
deceased Emperor should adorn his noble son, and
that whatever the new-fangled constitution of Diocletian might prescribe, his title should be not Caesar
but Augustus. Of the myriads of travellers who
hurry to and fro through the magnificent railway
station of York, how few find time to visit the
admirable museum of Roman antiquities which is
within a few hundred yards of the station, to gaze
upon the 'multangular tower' with its courses of
square Roman bricks, and in thought to retrace the
history of York, Eoforwic, Eboracum, up to that day
when the shouting soldiery, enraptured with the

donative which each man had received, acclaimed the young hero 'Constantine Imperator tu vincas.' Strange is it to reflect that then what we call 'the Eternal Eastern Question' had no existence, since he who was to give his name to Constantinople was only setting his foot on the first rung of the ladder of power, and the Bosphorus, with the inconsiderable city of Byzantium on its shores, was still a silent and solitary water-way, while Eboracum was making and unmaking Emperors.

Confusion and Civil War.

By the elevation of Constantine to the Imperial dignity—an elevation which Galerius found himself eventually forced to consent to—the whole of Diocletian's elaborate scheme of adoption, partnership and succession was shattered into atoms. The son of Maximian, Maxentius, followed the example of the son of Constantius and declared himself Augustus. Then old Maximian himself resumed the purple. In the year 308 there were six Emperors reigning at once, all styling themselves Augusti. Civil war in such conditions as these became the chronic condition of the Empire. The fable of the armed men who sprang from the dragon's teeth sown by Cadmus, and who fought with one another all the long summer's day till only five were left, became a terrible truth. Such was the scene, such the utter failure of his grand project for promoting the peace of the Empire upon which the weary eyes of Diocletian closed, when, seeking refuge in death from the indignities which his young successors would have put upon him, he passed away from earth in

Suicide of Diocletian, 313.

his stately palace by the Adriatic, that palace which in the Middle Ages became a city[1].

Of the dragon's brood of combatants, at the time of the death of Diocletian only two were left, Constantine in the West and Licinius in the East. A short civil war was terminated by an apparent reconciliation between the two kinsmen (Licinius had married the sister of Constantine), and for eight years Licinius seemed to be satisfied with an arrangement which left him only the Eastern quarter of the Roman world, while the Gauls, Italy and Illyricum obeyed his more fortunate and far abler rival. But

Constantine and Licinius, A 315.

> 'Never could true reconcilement grow,
>   Where wounds of deadly hate had pierced so deep.'

The terrible loneliness of those who climb to the high places of power, their incapacity of tolerating a rival near the throne produced the usual results, and in 323 the second civil war broke out. Over land and sea the two mighty storm-clouds moved with terrific momentum against one another. Thirty-four thousand men fell on the hardly-contested field of Hadrianople. Crispus, the brave young son of Constantine, forced the passage of the Dardanelles and laid siege to Byzantium. The final battle was fought in September, 323, at Chrysopolis in Bithynia. Licinius was defeated after a most bloody encounter, in which 25,000 of his followers were slain. He implored and seemed to receive the pardon of his 'Emperor and Master' Constantine, but in the following

Constantine sole ruler, 323.

---

[1] The city of Spalato now occupies the site of the palace of Diocletian, which was built in the neighbourhood of Salona.

year, on some suspicion of conspiracy, was put to death. Seventeen years after his being proclaimed at York, Constantine was sole and absolute master of the Roman world.

Christi-
anity and
the Em-
pire.

The generation which witnessed the break-down of Diocletian's scheme of adoptive succession witnessed also the final triumph of Christianity over its persecutors. By a somewhat undeserved fate, the name of the great restorer of the Empire has been handed down to after ages as that of the fiercest and most cruel of the oppressors of the Church. The

(303–313.)

persecution of the Christians which was commenced under Diocletian, and which continued, with some intermission, for the two last years of his reign and till the eighth year after his abdication, was not apparently originated by him, but by his younger and infinitely less statesmanlike colleague Galerius, who obtained the sanction indeed, but not the hearty co-operation of the aged and now valetudinarian Emperor. Still it must be admitted that Diocletian, though no fanatical adorer of the Olympian gods, believed in the necessity, on political grounds, of one great and relentless struggle for the suppression of the 'new and illicit religion' which had grown up in the bosom of the Roman State, and which, as all men of clear insight perceived, must either conquer it or be conquered by it.

Constan-
tine's atti-
tude to-
wards
Christi-
anity.

The same purely political instinct which made Diocletian persecute, led Constantine to foster and favour the Christian Church. Could we penetrate the secrets of the hearts of these two men, we might find that their religious convictions were not very dissimilar. Both were probably at heart Monotheists, both had that belief in a just and overruling Providence, which comes to most men who are in authority, and who, seeing the endless labour and contrivance which is needed in an earthly ruler to keep his world in any degree of order and peace, cannot easily persuade themselves that the whole of this fair system of things which we see around us came by chance. It may be doubted whether, in his heart of hearts, Diocletian went much beyond this position in his worship of Jupiter, or Constantine— at any rate till near the close of his life—in his belief in Christ. But the younger Emperor saw clearly that no fresh attempt to extirpate Christianity by force could succeed when Diocletian had failed; that the new religion made of its votaries not only better men, but, upon the whole, better citizens and more loyal subjects; that it possessed a force which, wisely guided, might be used for the preservation and not for the disruption of the Empire; above all, that the zealous partisanship of Christian bishops and priests would be a far more valuable ally to him in the desperate strife with his competitors—first with Maxentius and then with Licinius—than the languid half-hearted acquiescence of the Pagans in the religion which was a fashion rather than a faith, handed down to them from their forefathers.

Thus, then, the alliance of Constantine with the Christian Church was formed, that alliance of which the imposing Council of Nicaea, consisting of 318 bishops, presided over by the great Augustus himself, glorious in purple and gold, was the most conspicuous seal and symbol.   But though Constantine fostered, and, if I may so say, petted the Christian Church, he did not bring about that complete and intimate union of the State and the Church which was to be the distinguishing mark of the later, and pre-eminently of the Eastern Empire.   Christian ideas indeed coloured much of his legislation.   An edict was passed for the observance of 'the Saviour's day, the day of Light and of the Sun;' and the soldiers, even those who did not profess Christianity, were enjoined to meet on that day in some open space near the city in which they were quartered and to lift up their hands to heaven thanking God for past victories, and imploring Him long to preserve in safety and triumph their Emperor Constantine and his pious sons.   Every attempt to compel Christians to be present at idolatrous sacrifices was rigorously forbidden.   The more licentious of the heathen orgies were forcibly suppressed.   Many idol temples were thrown open to the gaze of the vulgar, and some were stripped of their treasures and their revenues for the benefit of the Imperial Treasury.

Still there was no formal renunciation of the worship of the gods of the Capitol—no formal recognition of Christianity as *the* religion of the Empire. The temples, though in some cases robbed of their gold and silver ornaments, remained standing; nay, even in the new and Christian capital, in Constantinople itself, new temples were erected, of course not

without the Emperor's cognisance, to Rhea, to the
Great Twin Brethren, to the Fortune of the New
Rome.

Two generations passed after the foundation of *Religious*
Constantinople, during which the relation of the *policy of*
Empire to the Christian Church was the central *tine's suc-*
question of all politics. These were the years during *cessors.*
which the strife between Athanasian and Arian was
being waged in all its bitterness, and the influence of
Constantius, the survivor of the sons of Constantine, and eventually the sole ruler of the Roman
Empire, was thrown with passionate earnestness
on the side of the Arians, on whose behalf he
exerted a severity which sometimes amounted to
actual persecution of their opponents. Then came
the short and fruitless attempt of Julian to restore
the worship of the old gods. After his death followed some further struggles with Arianism, which
could again boast the protection of an Eastern
Emperor[1]. All these events tended to bring the
supreme civil power more and more deeply into the
innermost circle of ecclesiastical politics. Men's
minds became familiarised with the idea of one
supreme and triumphant form of the Christian faith,
professed by the Emperor, inscribed on the forefront
of the State, and rigorously imposed on all citizens
as an essential condition of their citizenship. This
consummation was reached under that Emperor
whose fortunes I shall before long have to describe
to you, under Theodosius, who proclaimed the final

[1] Valens.

triumph of the Athanasian faith, commanded all his subjects to adhere to it, prohibited the meetings of heretics, destroyed the temples of the gods, and made orthodox Christianity, what it continued for more than a thousand years, the State religion of the Roman Empire.

LECTURE II.

THE ROMAN AND THE TEUTON.

————— •• —————

*Comparison of the Political and Social Condition of
the Empire and its German Neighbours.*

§ 1. THE ROMAN.

BEFORE I proceed to describe the collision between
the Roman Empire and its Northern neighbours,
I wish to sketch, in rapid outline, the chief features
of the political and social condition of these two
worlds, so close to one another in geographical
position, so far removed from one another in the
stages of their respective development.

We saw something in the last lecture of the pro- *The Im-*
cess by which the Roman Augustus had grown to *perial
Majesty.*
be what he was, the man with the mightiest oppor-
tunities for good or for evil of any on the surface of
our planet. Let us now look for a few minutes at
the outward presentation of this greatness to the
eyes of his subjects. If we enter the Imperial
palace and pass the first veil which guards the ante-
chamber of the sovereign we find ourselves at length
before a second veil, in front of which are watching
thirty *Silentiarii* in brightly burnished helmet and
breastplate, defending the 'Silence' of the innermost sanctuary from any rude intrusion. Without the

favour of some 'illustrious' functionary there would
be for us but little hope of entrance into that august
seclusion : but we who have travelled back over
fifteen centuries of time can push aside the spectral
Silentiarius who would forbid our entrance, and can
gaze, without the humiliating ceremony of prostration (exacted from all his contemporary subjects),
upon the face and figure of the dread Augustus.
He has perhaps just returned from the amphitheatre,
and wears therefore the full robes of royalty in which
he displays himself on state occasions to his subjects.
On his head is the diadem, a broad white band studded
with two rows of pearls, and with an emerald or a
carbuncle blazing in the centre.   Jewelled ear-rings
hang down on either side of his face.   Over his
shoulders is hung a purple robe, richly embroidered
with gold, similar to the *vestis picta* which a conquering general used to wear in old times when he
was drawn in triumph to the Capitol.   The use of
that purple colour is now jealously reserved to the
Emperor himself, the members of the Imperial
family, the Consuls, and a few of the most highly
placed officers of state.   For any ordinary subject
to wear it would be an act of *laesa majestas* (high
treason).   More than once has a Roman citizen lost
his life, simply because a purple robe has been
found in his possession.   Upon his feet the Emperor
wears sandals of the same purple dye, and these
also are richly studded with jewels.

In the midst of all this pomp, though sleek
eunuchs and brilliantly dressed pages are moving

obsequiously through the chamber, eager to anticipate the slightest wish of their master, the Lord of
the Universe does not present the outward show
of happiness. There is a look of weariness and
anxiety in his face, dark lines under his eyes,
languor and satiety in the very tones of his voice.
Though there are some exceptions to the rule, the
Augustus, since the changes introduced by Diocletian, leads generally an indoor life, unfavourable to
health. He does not take those long and varied
journeys which filled up the life of Hadrian: he
does not, except in dire necessity, march at the head
of his troops like Trajan: he does not even drive
chariots and contend for prizes in the theatre like
Nero. He has now to keep himself aloof from his
subjects in dignified seclusion: his chief business in
life is to be worshipped: and the life of an idol
must, as it seems to us, be always a tedious life.
The one thing that varies the monotony of the
slowly-pacing days is fear—that fear which, even
under this new and more settled order of things, no
Emperor can wholly banish from his mind—that in
some camp of misty Britain, or by the mob of some
Syrian city, a rival Augustus may be suddenly acclaimed, and that it may be necessary to struggle
not for dominion only but for bare life against the
desperate antagonist.

The being who dwelt in this stately seclusion was *Deification*
not only raised to the ranks of the gods after his *of the Em-*
death ('*Divus*' being the regular official prefix of *peror.*
the name of a deceased Emperor): he was occasion-

ally even addressed as '*Deus Noster*,' 'our God,'
during his life. '*Dominus Noster*,' 'our Lord' or
'our Master,' was, however, his more usual title,
this appellation which the modesty of Augustus had
waived (since, as he said, it implied that those who
used it were his slaves) having been freely accepted,
and then jealously claimed, by his successors of the
Lower Empire. Everything belonging to the Emperor was habitually, and without any trace of irony,
spoken of as 'Sacred.' The 'sacred bedchamber'
meant the Emperor's bedroom: the 'sacred largesses,' the Imperial subscription-list. 'Our Mild-
ness,' 'our Tranquillity,' 'our Clemency,' are the
terms which the Emperors generally use when they
are speaking of themselves, though occasionally we
find an Emperor soaring even to higher regions of
august self-contemplation and speaking of himself as
'my Eternity[1].' This reverential mode of speaking
of the Emperor's dignity by no means disappeared
with the adoption of Christianity. A writer on
military affairs, who was probably contemporary with
Theodosius[2], says of the oath taken by the army:
'The soldiers swear by God and Christ and the
Holy Spirit, and by the Majesty of the Emperor,
which, according to the will of God, is to be loved
and worshipped by the human race. For when the
Emperor has received the name of Augustus, faithful devotion is to be rendered, lifelong service is to

[1] Cod. Theod. xii. 1, 160. It is Arcadius who uses this expression.

[2] Vegetius (De Re Militari ii. 5).

be paid, to him as to God present in a human body[1].
For that man, whether soldier or civilian, serves
God who faithfully loves him who reigns by God's
ordinance.'

In one of the apartments of the palace was assem- *The Impe-*
bled the *Consistory* of the Emperor, a body some- *rial Con-*
sistory.
what resembling our Privy Council, and consisting
of all the highest officials of the State. From this
Consistory now went forth all laws, addressed in the
Emperor's name to some great functionary charged
to see to their execution. Here, too, were announced
the names of those persons whom the Emperor
nominated to the highest places in the civil and
military service. All this legislative and administrative work, which in the days of the Republic had
required the concurrence of the Senate and People
of Rome, and a large share of which had been left
even by Augustus and Tiberius to the Senate, was
now done by the mere *fiat* of the Emperor; and only
slight traces of even a theoretical right of confirmation by the Senate, none at all of such a right of
confirmation by the People, seem to have been
preserved.

The officials, civil and military, by whom the work *Three*
of ruling the vast Roman Empire was carried on, *classes in*
the Impe-
were divided into three great classes:— *rial hier-*
archy.
    1. The *Illustres*, nearly corresponding to our
Cabinet Ministers and Commander-in-Chief.

----

[1] 'Nam imperator cum Augusti nomen accepit, tanquam prae-
senti et corporali Deo fidelis est praestanda devotio, inpendendus
pervigil famulatus.'

2. The *Spectabiles*, whose rank was not unlike that of our Privy Councillors, and who included most of the governors of provinces and military officers of rank.

3. The *Clarissimi.* This title was given to all Senators, and was also shared by some of the governors of provinces of inferior rank, and subordinate commissioned officers.

The No-titia.

The various degrees and orders of this great official hierarchy were accurately described in a treatise called the *Notitia Utriusque Imperii,* which, there is some reason to think, was written up by each Emperor afresh on his accession to the throne. This document is illustrated by somewhat grotesque pictures, emblematic of the contents of the various chapters, which may have been drawn by the unskilful fingers of the Imperial scribe. The copies of the *Notitia* which we possess describe the state of things existing about the beginning of the fifth century, and bring before us in a wonderful manner the various and skilfully contrived channels by which, in theory at least, the great Imperial power flowed down to, and was brought in contact with, the meanest of its subjects. The first chapter enumerates all the chief officers of the Eastern Empire. The second takes up the office of the PRAETORIAN PREFECT, greatest of all the Illustres, a man who, after his office had undergone great mutations, had at length become, so to speak, the Grand Vizier of the Emperor, his *alter ego* and vicegerent, the official who took as much as possible

of the drudgery of ruling off the shoulders of a
monarch, who, if ill-disposed, wanted to take his
fill of luxury and sensual enjoyment, or if earnest to
perform the duties of his station, was generally busy
on the frontier, warring with the barbarians.

Though the scheme of Diocletian for 'adoptive
succession, and partnership' had broken down, his
skilful division of the vast spaces of the Empire still
endured, and each one of the four Prefectures
founded by him was still under the rule of its own
special Praetorian Prefect. This second chapter,
then, of the *Notitia* describes the various provincial
governors, who are, in its phrase, 'under the disposition' of the Illustrious Praetorian Prefect of
the East. Then follows an enumeration of the
official staff—the registrars, the shorthand-writers,
the process-servers, the beadles, the gaolers who
were employed in the court of the Praetorian Prefect, himself not merely a great Minister of State,
but also the highest Judge of Appeal, Premier, and
Lord Chancellor in one.

Another chapter of the *Notitia* gives the emblems *Magister*
of the dignity of the Illustrious MASTER OF THE *Militiae.*
SOLDIERY in the East, and enumerates the various
legions which were under his disposition. And
here we are brought face to face with the interesting question, What was the size of the Roman army *Probable*
at the time when its greatest struggle with the bar- *size of the*
barians began? Unfortunately the *Notitia*, though *army.*
it gives us much detailed information as to the
disposition of various bodies of infantry and cavalry,

does not enable us to give a definite answer to this question ; and unfortunately also an impression has been produced, one can hardly tell how, that by this time the Legion, the well-known unit of computation in the Roman army, had been formally reduced from its old strength of 6100 men to about 1000. Of course this suggestion throws all calculations as to the size of the army, derived from the number of legions contained in it, into confusion. But as no proof of this formal reduction of the legion has yet been offered, I prefer to take it at its old valuation : and so doing, I come to the conclusion that the Roman army at the end of the fourth century consisted on paper of at least 950,000 men[1]. To deduce from this its actual effective strength can be only a matter of conjecture ; but my conjecture would be that fully one-half of the above number, or 475,000 men, were at that time serving under the banners of the Empire[2].

[1] The Computation proceeds in this way. The *Notitia* enumerates 132 'Legions' of foot soldiers and 109 other bodies of infantry, 'Numeri,' 'Auxilia,' and so forth, whose precise strength we cannot ascertain: also 91 'Vexillationes,' 'Alae,' &c., of cavalry.

Taking the 132 Legions at 6100 men we get .	805,200
Taking the 109 Numeri, &c. at 1000 we get .	109,000
Taking the 91 Vexillationes at 600 (the full number of a Vexillatio) we get . .	54,600
	968,800

[2] There is an interesting passage in the Greek historian Agathias (who wrote about 570) which illustrates, if it does not precisely confirm the view here taken. He says (Hist. v. 13): 'The armies of the Romans no longer remained of the size at which they had

If I am not wearying you, we will turn over a few more pages of this wonderful handbook, which I have often in my own mind compared to a *Whitaker's Almanack* and an *Army List* for the fifth century after Christ, bound up together. Even that comparison hardly does justice to the *Notitia*. I doubt if we have any book which in our own country shows so clearly and so concisely the relations of the various departments of our State to one another (for instance, of the Exchequer to the Treasury, or of the Privy Council to the Poor Law Board) as this treatise shows the functions of the great officers of the Roman State and the classes of civil servants over whom they bore sway. After the Master of the Soldiery, that is, the Commander-in-Chief, we come to the Illustrious Grand Chamberlain, or, as he was called in the high-flown language of the Court, the SUPERINTENDENT OF THE SACRED CUBICLE. Our MSS. of the *Notitia* are defective in the chapters relating to this magnificent personage, but we know from other sources that he ruled over an army of pages, scullions, keepers of the

Praepositus Sacri Cubiculi.

been originally fixed by the earlier Emperors, but had dwindled down to a tiny remnant, by no means adequate to the size of the State. For whereas they ought to amount in the whole to 645,000 warlike men, they have been now reduced to little more than 150,000.' As Agathias wrote under Justinian, after the greater part of the West had been lost to the Empire, he probably reduced his figures of 'paper-strength' and 'effectives' in proportion to the diminution of the Empire; and if so, he would probably have accepted for the year 400, when the territories of the sons of Theodosius were still intact, a result like that mentioned in the text.

wardrobe, grooms of the bedchamber, and the like, and that the thirty gleaming *Silentiarii* who watched outside the purple veil took their orders from him.

Magister Officiorum.

The Illustrious MASTER OF THE OFFICES is next described. In a quaint picture are represented the emblems of his rank, a table with the likeness of the Emperor standing upon it, and underneath shields, spears, greaves and helmets. We learn from the text that the arsenals of the Empire, the Postal Service, the four great bureaux[1] which were responsible for the Imperial correspondence and for receiving and answering petitions, the swarm of King's Messengers (as they would now be called) or *Agentes in Rebus*, who rode up and down through the provinces, executing the orders of the Sovereign, were all under the disposition of this hard-worked and useful functionary.

Quaestor.

The Illustrious QUAESTOR was responsible for the preparation of the Emperor's Edicts, and seems to have shared with the Master of the Offices the duty of replying to the humble petitions of his subjects. A bundle of these petitions and a box, which looks like a pillar post-office, inscribed 'Leges Salutares,' appear on his page of the *Notitia* among the emblems of the Quaestor's dignity.

Comes Sacrarum Largitionum.

Comes Privatarum Rerum.

The Illustrious COUNT OF THE SACRED LARGESSES and COUNT OF THE PRIVATE DOMAINS were the two great financial ministers of the State. Theoretically the first might have been expected to discharge only the duties of a Grand Almoner, in supervising the

---

[1] Scrinia.

Imperial Charities. Practically, however, he had to superintend the collection of revenue from Illyrian silver mines and Egyptian corn-fields, from the manufacturers of linen, and the traders in salt. The Count of the Private Domains similarly superintended the vast estates belonging to the Crown in the various provinces of the Empire, defended them from squatters, urged the claims of his sovereign to the land of a subject dying without natural heirs, and received the reports of the stud-masters who watched over the troops of horses reared for the Emperor in the plains of Thrace and Cappadocia. The pictures denoting the functions of these two officers are nearly alike, both representing money-chests, sacks fat with gold and silver, and great bowls filled with round masses of bullion.

Such is a very brief outline of the system of *Merits and* civil and military administration as arranged by *defects of the Impe-* Diocletian and Constantine. This bureaucracy (I *rial Bu-* know no pure English word which expresses the *reaucracy.* idea) carried on the government of the Eastern Empire for more than a thousand years. It had great faults—it was grasping, repressive, too often corrupt. At the beginning of the fifth century, if we may believe a poet of the Opposition[1], an Eunuch, who by Imperial favour had climbed up into the high place of Praetorian Prefect, dared to open an auction mart in his private chamber for the actual sale of provincial governorships to the highest bidder. And even where there was

[1] Claudian.

not positive corruption, there can be little doubt
that the rule of the Byzantine officials was generally impoverishing and exhausting to the provinces, paying but little heed to their just complaints,
and bent on screwing out of them the uttermost
farthing for the Emperor, if not for the officials'
own private benefit. Still the officialism of the
Empire had some great merits, without which it
could never have subsisted so long as it did. The
regular gradation of offices, the scientific division
of powers, the career opened by the civil service
to intellect, irrespective of noble birth or warlike
prowess—all these things made of the administrative hierarchy of the Roman Empire a great engine
of civilisation in those dim mediaeval centuries,
and one which contrasted favourably in many respects with the rough barbaric forces that were
everywhere else struggling for supremacy. If the
student wishes to know how it was that the Empire of Constantine, notwithstanding all its degene-
racy, lasted on in the East for 1120 years, let him
study that curious and interesting document, the
Notitia Imperii.

*Social con-
dition of
the Em-
pire.*

Passing from the political, I will make a few
remarks on the social state of the Empire in the
fourth century after Christ. Our information on
this subject is very imperfect. We have no authors
who, like the comedians of Athens, or like Horace
and Juvenal in Rome, enable us to reconstruct a
picture of the manners and customs of those far-
off times, almost as vivid as is furnished by the

Miss Austens and the Anthony Trollopes of the
nineteenth century. Still we have something. Ammianus Marcellinus, the great historian of Julian
and Valentinian, possessed the eye and hand of a
satirist ; and St. Jerome, even in denouncing the
vices of fashionable society in Rome, brings us into
nearer acquaintance with its good as well as its evil
qualities.

Taking a broad survey, we may say that the *Division*
characteristic of Roman social life in the later *between*
Empire, was the gulf (a far wider and more bridge- *classes.*
less gulf than exists in our own day) between the
very rich and the very poor. The Roman did not
take naturally either to manufacturing or to retail
shop-keeping. He was (perhaps I should rather
say, he had been) essentially a warrior. The rich
Roman was still lawyer, civil servant, money-lender,
and land owner. The poor Roman was tiller of the
soil—often under very hard conditions—or else
'loafer' (no other word will express my meaning)
in the cities. What was true of the dweller in Rome
was true also to some extent of the Romanised
population of the provinces. Now, if we consider
what these statements amount to, and if we consider
also the invariable influence of slavery in crushing
out the better class of free artisans, we shall see that
we have here a society from which the middle class
and the more independent portion of the lower class
are perpetually tending to disappear ; in other words,
a society composed of the very rich and of the
employés of the State at one end, and of the pro-

letariat[1] at the other, with only weak and insufficient padding between.

We have some interesting information as to the fortunes of wealthy Romans about the year 420, after the distress caused by the invasion of the barbarians had begun. In the first families in Rome it was not unusual for the master of the household to have an income of £160,000 a year, besides the produce of vine-yards and corn-lands, which was worth quite £50,000 more[2]. Wealthy families of the second class were worth from £40,000 to £60,000 a year. A Senator named Probus, when his son was made Praetor about 423, spent £48,000 on the shows which it was still customary for that functionary to exhibit to the people. Some fifteen years before, ere Rome had yet been taken by the barbarians, Symmachus the orator, a man who was deemed to possess only a moderate fortune, had spent £80,000 on similar exhibitions;

[1] Though this word has lately obtained, chiefly through the influence of French writers, rather too wide currency, as the polite equivalent of 'mob,' a writer on Roman affairs may with better right employ it, as it is derived from the politics of old Rome. In the *Comitia Centuriata*, the lowest class of citizens, those who were assessed on a very small amount of property, and who had little beside their children (*proles*) wherewith to serve the State, were called *proletarii*. The word seems to have passed out of use before the close of the Republic.

[2] In this sentence and throughout these lectures I quote actual sums of money, without attempting to make any correction for the alteration in its value, that being an element extremely difficult to calculate. There is no doubt that the purchasing power of the equivalent of £1 sterling was greater then than now, how much greater it is almost impossible to say, I conjecture about double.

while Maximus, who was considered one of the very rich citizens of Rome, lavished £160,000 upon the festivities, which, notwithstanding this prodigious expenditure, only lasted seven days. At this time the palace of every Roman nobleman had spacious baths, forum, hippodrome, fountains, temples (or churches) within its enclosure, so that a stranger visiting Rome cried out with enthusiasm

'Every house is a town, Rome holds a myriad of cities.'

St. Jerome tells us that the devout lady Paula, who claimed descent on the paternal side from Agamemnon, and on the maternal from the Scipios, was possessed of vast wealth, and that the whole city of Nicopolis (founded by Augustus to commemorate the battle of Actium) belonged to her alone.

The men who owned these enormous fortunes seemed to Ammianus to be for the most part cold-hearted and effeminate dandies, unworthy of the great name of Rome, whose foremost citizens they were. A lofty chariot would be one man's sign of distinction, another covered himself with a multitude of cloaks of finest silken texture, each one fastened round his neck by a jewelled clasp, and perpetually wriggled his body about or waved his hand in order to call the attention of the bystanders to the gay fringes of his robe or the figures of animals embroidered upon it in divers colours of needle-work. Others strutted along the street followed by a whole army of retainers, and when they entered the public baths attended by at least fifty slaves, at once began

Habits of wealthy Romans.

to shout out in a voice that was meant to strike awe
into all humbler visitors, 'Where are my people?'
A contemptuous toss of the head was all that they
vouchsafed to an acquaintance ; to the fawning
flatterer who was hungering for their smile they
would contemptuously offer a hand or a knee to
kiss.   But all this affectation of aristocratic *hauteur*
vanished when some woman of doubtful reputation
drew near, or when news was brought to them of
the arrival of some fresh horses or charioteers of
extraordinary skill.   The banquet was to these men
a time of dull and solemn sensuality.   When the
panting slave placed on the table a fish or a turkey
of unusual size, they would send for the scales and
order it to be weighed, and then one of the crowd of
hungry secretaries standing by would be called upon
to record the prodigy on his tablets.   Beyond this
kind of employment for the pen, their ideas either of
literature or of science hardly soared.

The poorer
citizens of
Rome.

Thus empty and frivolous appeared to a contemporary satirist the lives of the Roman nobility.
Of the lives of the poorer citizens he gives us fewer
details, but we can see that for them as for their
ancestors the interest of life was summed up in three
words *'Panem et Circenses'*—bread and circus-shows.
By a well-understood bargain between the Roman
mob and the Roman Emperor—a bargain which
lasted through all the centuries from Julius to Augus-
tulus—he was bound to provide them with at least
food enough to keep them from starving, and with a
proper amount of excitement in the form of games,

chariot races, and fights of gladiators and wild beasts; and if he failed in this, the first duty of a ruler, his diadem and his life were both forfeit. The elaborate provisions of the Theodosian code *Bread dis-* enable us to understand how the duty of feeding the *tribution.* mob was performed. We see the householders of Rome seated on broad flights of stairs throughout the fourteen regions of the City, and receiving from the slaves who obeyed the orders of the Super-intendent of Supply (*Praefectus Annonae*) their loaves of fine wheaten flour, each weighing about a pound and a half[1], and in addition, a certain quantity of oil.

And then as to the games. The history of Am- *Games.* mianus and the letters of Cassiodorus show us these same unemployed citizens flocking to the stately Colosseum, or the spacious Hippodrome, and shout-ing themselves hoarse with the name of some favourite gladiator or charioteer. The chariot races especially, stirred the people to a frenzy of excite-ment, surpassing that of a contested election or an Irish faction-fight. The two colours, blue and green, flaunted by one set of charioteers or the other, stirred the citizens both of Rome and Con-stantinople to the very madness of triumph or disappointment. 'The green charioteer flashes by: part of the people is in despair. The blue gets ahead: a larger part of the city is in misery. They cheer frantically when they have gained nothing:

[1] Perhaps the ration was proportioned to the size of the receiver's family, but this we cannot say with certainty.

they are cut to the heart when they have received no loss : and they plunge with as much eagerness into these empty contests as if the whole welfare of the imperilled fatherland was at stake [1].'

In such a round of ignoble excitements, in such an attitude of dishonourable dependence on the feeding power of the State—pauperism disguised under high-sounding names—the mob of Rome and of Constantinople, apparently also of Antioch and Alexandria, spent their lazy lives. Meanwhile the agricultural population and the inhabitants of the smaller provincial towns were daily sinking lower into the gulf of hopeless poverty, toiling, yet scarce able with all their labour to keep famine from their doors. At the base of the social pyramid were of *Slave-system.* course to be found the Slaves, those unhappy beings who, shut up at night in the huge and gloomy *ergastula* (slave-barracks), worked all day under the hot Italian sun, cultivating the land of some wealthy master, unknown, unseen, only represented by a hard, relentless *villicus* (steward), himself a slave, but delighting to make the more miserable creatures under him feel his power. These were the kind of establishments which, a hundred years or more before the Republic fell, had replaced the happy homesteads of the Latin or Sabine farmer : and it was the sight of this spreading plague-spot of servile agriculture which in the first century of the Christian era forced from Pliny the well-known cry of lamentation, 'Large estates have been the ruin of

[1] Cassiodorus, Variarum iii. 51.

Italy and are now causing the ruin of the provinces[1].' Yet perhaps in the fifth century the slave
was not the most miserable of the rural inhabitants.
Christianity had already introduced some betterment
into his condition. The *ergastulum* was prohibited
by law, if we may not think that it had entirely disappeared in fact : and decrees were beginning to be
issued, earnestly protesting against that breaking up
of families which is one of the most cruel characteristics of predial slavery[2]. And at any rate the
slave, in all ordinary circumstances, was safe from
death by starvation, a security which was not always
enjoyed by his social superiors.

Next above the slave, and often hardly to be dis- *Coloni.*
tinguished from him, was the *colonus* or serf, a man
over whom his lord had no power of life and death,
but who was bound—as were his children after
him—to cultivate a particular piece of ground for
the owner, at a rent which seems to have been
practically unchanged from generation to generation.
He had therefore no power of changing his condition nor of choosing a better landlord, but on the
other hand he had practically a kind of tenant-
right which he transmitted, with the corresponding

[1] 'Verumque confitentibus latifundia perdidere Italiam : jam vero
et provincias. Sex domini semissem Africae possidebant, cum
interfecit eos Nero princeps.' Hist. Nat. xviii. 6.

[2] Cod. Theod. ii. 25. 'Quis enim ferat, liberos a parentibus, a
fratribus sorores, a viris conjuges segregari?' The date of this law
is not quite certain, but it probably belongs to A.D. 334. There is
no doubt that Constantine was the author of it, and we may therefore
fairly attribute it to Christian influences.

liability, to his children. This class of compulsory
cultivators seems to have sprung out of freeholders
who were weighed down by hopeless debt, and who
by process of law became *coloni* of their creditors[1];
but it was probably enormously increased during
the troubles of the third and fourth centuries, when
men finding freedom with starvation a burden too
heavy to be borne, voluntarily lowered their condition, and becoming *coloni* accepted the helping but
degrading hand of a *dominus*. In times of peace and
plenty the condition of a *colonus*, notwithstanding
his bounded horizon and his depressing round of
unvarying toil, was perhaps not altogether to be
pitied : but war, famine, and pestilence must have
terribly reduced his narrow margin of profit.

Curiales.   Of all classes of the community, however, none
seem to me so truly to be commiserated as the
curiales, the vestrymen and town-councillors of the
provinces. These were the descendants of the men
by whom the local self-government of the Empire
had formerly been carried on, the representatives of
a once flourishing and happy middle class. Their
ancestors had been men of importance in their little
world, and the letters D E C (for Decurio, or town-
councillor) carved on their tombs had shown their
right to a coveted dignity. But as they bore rule
in their little commonwealth, so they were responsible for its contributions to the public revenue ; and
as the Empire grew older, as it became divided, as
there came to be three or four Imperial Courts to

[1] See Fustel de Coulanges, Problèmes de l'Histoire.

support instead of one, and as heavier sums had to
be paid to buy off or to fight off the barbarians, so
the pressure of the tax-gatherer became more severe,
while the privileges of the town-councillor became
more shadowy. At last the truth was openly confessed : the *curialis* was a mere bond-slave of the
Empire, bound to fulfil his 'curial obligations,' that
is, to bear an ever-increasing burden of local rates
and imperial taxes, transmitting this sad necessity to
his children, compelled if the land next to him fell
out of cultivation to take it up and cultivate it for the
benefit of the Imperial Treasury, forbidden to become
a priest or even a slave, lest by either process he
might escape from his bondage to the *curia.* One or
two ways of escape from this bitter servitude were
indeed left open, but they were narrow, thorny, and
difficult. Practically the chief liberator of the *curialis* and his kindest friend was Death.

The sketch which I have thus offered you of the
social condition of the Empire in the fourth century
is certainly a gloomy one. Like all such sketches it
can only be approximately true. Doubtless there
were at Rome many nobles unlike the effeminate
dandies whom Ammianus has described to us :
doubtless there was in the provinces many a cul-
tivator of the soil, whether *colonus* or *curialis,* who
glided happily enough through life, not crushed by
the burdens and the despairs which seem to us so
terrible. Yes : though I cannot accept the proposition that the sum of human happiness is a constant
quantity throughout the centuries, I doubt not that

in the saddest periods of the history of the world there has been more individual happiness, and in the happiest of such periods more individual suffering, than the historian pourtrays to us. But upon the whole we may confidently say that the Roman World, at the time when the barbarian invasion began in earnest, was not happy or flourishing. Large tracts of land within the *Limes Imperii* were going out of cultivation, population both in Italy and the provinces was dwindling, and I think Hope was unusually absent from the hearts and minds of men. In short, the Empire was sinking under the weight of its official administration, even as I fear that after ages will see that many fair states of Europe are now sinking under the weight of the terrible armaments with which mutual suspicion has led them to array themselves.

§ 2. THE TEUTON.

From the highly-developed life of the Empire, with its signs of exhaustion and decay, we turn to that of our German forefathers and their kindred—a life rough, untrained, undisciplined, but already utterly different from that of mere savages, and bearing within it the seeds of many noble institutions. The German peoples (to speak of them in the language of Rome), the *Deutsche* (as they have in more recent times called themselves), or the Teutonic[1] race (which is the term

[1] Waitz (Deutsche Verfassungsgeschichte i. 30) remarks that

now generally used in contrast to Celts and Slaves), occupied, broadly speaking, the territory from the Rhine to the Danube, and along the northern shore of the Danube to the Black Sea. There were settlements, however, of the Teutons on the west of the Rhine, and in the east of Europe Sclavonic nations were mingled with Teutons in a confusion which it is now impossible to disentangle. Of their ethnological relations, however, I shall have a little more to say in my next lecture. At present my object is to give a slight sketch of the inner life of these Teutonic peoples, in its social and political aspects.

The first detailed information that we possess as to the customs of the Germans is given us by Julius Caesar, who describes the state of things which prevailed about 55 years before Christ. Our next and by far our fullest information comes from Tacitus, who wrote his priceless monograph, the *Germania*, in 98 A.D., that is, about a century and a half after Caesar. During that interval it is clear that an important change had come over the habits of the Germans. From being a pastoral people, living chiefly on milk and cheese and the flesh of their cattle, they had become, to a large extent, tillers of the soil. They still kept their flocks and herds, and wealth among them was still measured chiefly by these possessions; but

The Germans at the end of the first century after Christ not a nomadic people.

'Teutonic' and 'Deutsch' have probably no connection with one another.

bread was now a staple article of food, and perhaps that upon which the slaves and the poorer
freemen chiefly subsisted. This change in diet
involved a necessary change in the habits of the
people. The shepherd and the herdsman are
essentially wanderers; the varied needs of their
dumb companions in winter and summer, make
frequent change of abode not only easy but profit-
able, while the agriculturist of course must remain stationary to watch the growth of the corn
which he has sown. It seems probable that
Caesar's conquest of Gaul, Tiberius's victories in
Switzerland and the Tyrol, and the strong re-
straining hand of Augustus upon all the tribes
beyond the Rhine and the Danube, were partly
the cause of this change in the habits of the Germans. Cooped within narrower limits, and no
longer able to overrun at their pleasure the fair
lands of Gaul and Pannonia, they betook themselves of necessity to a more careful cultivation of
their restricted territory, and practised the arts of a
rude husbandry—rude indeed, but incomparably less
wasteful of the earth's resources than the nomadic
life of the grazier and the sheep-master. In its
turn this change in their habits reacted on their
character. It made the maintenance of peace between them and the Empire possible for two or three
generations at a time, and it so far fixed the bounds
of the habitations of the Germanic peoples themselves, that the map of Germany which is drawn
to illustrate the text of Tacitus will serve, without

many changes, for the distribution of the tribes in
the time of Constantine.

Let us try to understand what the life of these *A German*
German farmers looked like in a time of peace during *village-*
settlement.
the second and third centuries of the Christian era.
Their settlements, like those of a Canadian back-
woodsman, were for the most part clearings in the
midst of 'the forest primeval.' Here, then, with a
girdle of woodland round them, was planted the
cluster of scattered houses which made up the village. The Romans called it a *vicus*, the modern
Germans call it a *dorf* (a word akin to our own *thorp*);
our Saxon and Anglian ancestors called it sometimes a *ton*[1] (town), sometimes a *ham*[2]; while their
Danish invaders gave to the same kind of settlement
the name of a *by* or a *wick*[3]. The houses in the
German village were built of timber, and if Tacitus
is correct in saying that tiles were unknown among
them, we must, I suppose, conclude that the straw
thatches which are still common in rural England
were the roofs chiefly used by our German ancestors.
One feature of a German village which struck the
eye of a Roman observer, and in which it probably
differed even from a Celtic town, was that there were
in it no rows of contiguous houses. Each dwelling,

[1] Norton, Sutton, Easton, Weston, &c.

[2] Laleham, Farnham, Tottenham, &c., but more often with
a genitive plural preceding it. Birmingham (the village of the
Beormings), Buckingham (the village of the Bucings), and
so on.

[3] Derby, Danby, Whitby, &c.; Elswick, Alnwick, Chiswick, &c.

whether large or small, stood surrounded by its own
plot of ground, and thus fires were less dangerous
than where the lines of buildings were continuous.
The description of such a *vicus* given by Tacitus
reminds one of a Swiss village, say Meyringen,
Grindelwald, or Altdorf, if we can imagine all the
changes which have been wrought therein by the
tide of summer tourists done away.   And the great
belt of woodland which seems always to have surrounded the German *vicus*, and which was to a
certain extent the common property of the villagers,
who possessed rights of collecting fuel, and probably
also of hunting game in these encircling forests,
reminds me of several modern German villages
which I have seen, but especially of Schwalbach,
which is environed by just such a belt of trees,
chiefly beech-trees.   In this beautiful green girdle,
which is from one to two miles in depth, the poor
of the village are still employed during the winter in
felling and carrying wood for the benefit of the
Gemeinde, and the wages paid to them for this work
seem to supply the place of what is called with us
' out-door relief.'

Distinction   In these little sequestered villages the bulk of the
of classes in   German warriors had their homes.   There was a
a German
village.   distinction of classes among them.   Then, as now,
the German looked upon noble birth with reverence,
and probably in every village there were at least one
or two heads of families called noble, and believed
to be sprung in far-distant ages from the seed of
gods.   But the largest and most important class was

that of the men, free but not noble[1], who took part
in all public assemblies, and who formed the bone
and muscle of the national army, but who, though
proud and independent, did not look upon themselves as eligible for any of the highest places in the
State.   Among these, however, there were all sorts
of gradations of rank, depending partly on personal
qualities, but largely also on their relative wealth.
The chief outward sign of this wealth was cattle, so
much so that the earliest translator of the New
Testament into a Teutonic tongue coined a word
equivalent to 'cattle-hoarder[2],' when he wished to
warn his readers against the 'mammon of unrighteous-
ness.'   But slaves also were possessed, probably in
considerable numbers, by wealthy German villagers,
though they were employed almost entirely in the
labour of the farm and the pasture, all domestic work
being as a rule performed by the female members
of even the rich German family.   Half-naked, and
far from clean, the children of the master and of the
slave sprawled about together on the floor of either
home, until the years of manhood were reached,
when it was deemed fitting that some distinctive dress
should show the difference of their rank.   But it was
in these smoky huts, on these dirty floors, and
doubtless also in many a long day's chase along
with the slave-boys in the encircling forest, that

---

[1] The *Ingenui* of the Latin writers: the *Gemein-freie* of modern
Germans.

[2] *Faihu-thrains* (literally cattle-thronging) is Ulfilas' translation
of Μαμμωνᾶς.

the fair limbs of the young German warriors grew
to that size and that sinewy stateliness which, as
Tacitus admits, were the admiration and the terror
of Rome.

Land-sys-
tem of the
Germans.

[1] The agriculture of these Teutonic tribes was conducted in a manner which necessarily kept it in a
backward and primitive state. Apparently the Germans had learnt the lesson that frequent grain-crops
exhaust the fertility of the soil. Anything like a
scientific system of manuring, in order to repair that
exhausted fertility, was of course yet undiscovered ;
but a rude provision for fallows seems to have been
generally made. Periodically, the whole population
of the village went forth into the adjacent country
and decided upon the portion of pasture or moorland
which was to be broken up by the plough in order to
replace the portion of arable land which had earned
the right to repose. The new corn-land thus created
was divided among the villagers, not equally, but
according to their rank and wealth, chiefly because

[1] This paragraph is an attempt to explain the following passage
of Tacitus (Germania xxvi) which has been almost as much
fought over by commentators as if it had been a text of Scrip-
ture:—

'Agri pro numero cultorum ab universis in vices occupantur, quos
mox inter se secundum dignationem partiuntur. Facilitatem parti-
endi camporum spatia praestant. Arva per annos mutant; et superest ager.'

I follow in some points the interpretation given by Waitz
(Deutsche Verfassungsgeschichte i. 109-113 and 140-148), and
Dahn (Geschichte der deutschen Urzeit i. 171-174) ; but on the
whole the criticism of Fustel de Coulanges (Problèmes d'Histoire,
263-294) seems to me to penetrate most deeply into the author's
meaning.

rank and wealth implied a proportionate power of
cultivation [1]. While the poor freeman, who was
only just above the rank of a slave, could bring only
his own arms and those of his sons to till the little
patch of ground which was allotted to him, his
wealthy neighbour, who had slaves and horses and
herds in abundance, could cultivate, and therefore
might insist upon having allotted to him, a much
larger part of the new corn-land. Thus, by this
arrangement, as by so many of those which belong
to a more complicated civilisation, 'to him that had,
more was given, so that he had abundance.' After
all, every German village had still so much land
at its disposal, that few heartburnings seem to have
been caused on the score of too scanty allotment [2].
And in order to prevent the complaint that one
villager received a more fertile or a sunnier portion
than another, the lots periodically [3], perhaps even
annually, changed hands, though still on the same
principle of unequal division.

At first sight, such a system as this appears com-
munistic, but on reflexion we see that the right of
property, and the inequalities which flow from the
acknowledgment of that right, are fully recognised
by it. Only I think we must admit—and here the
words both of Caesar [4] and Tacitus seem to justify

[1] 'Secundum dignationem partiuntur.'

[2] 'Et superest ager.'

[3] 'Arva per annos mutant.' Perhaps this is meant to convey a
different meaning from 'per annum.'

[4] De Bello Gallico, iv. 1, vi. 22.

our conclusion—that there was in the minds of the rough German politicians of the first century before and the first century after Christ, a conviction, or perhaps rather an instinct, that the land, though still cheap and not much more an object of desire than water or air, was, like water and air, essential to the nation's life; and that, though cottages and the surrounding gardens were the subject of absolute property, and descended from father to son without question, it was safer for the community by frequent changes to prevent the right of any one of its members to a given space of corn-land or meadow from becoming firm and immovable.

How these open fields were probably divided into strips, or 'yard-lands'; how the villagers sometimes helped one another in the necessary ploughing; how some traces of this peculiar kind of joint occupation existed through the Middle Ages, and were still manifest in our own country even in the early part of this century, has been set forth with much fulness of detail by my friend Mr. Seebohm, in his interesting book, *The English Village Community*[1].

Indolence of the Germans.

Whatever other advantages this system might possess, it was not likely to encourage highly-developed agriculture. But indeed, from the account given by

---

[1] The strongest part of Mr. Seebohm's book is, I think, his illustration of the old Teutonic land-tenure by the open fields now or lately existing at Hitchin. I confess I am not convinced by him that the open field system and 'co-aration' necessarily imply a servile tenure on the part of the cultivators.

Tacitus, which is generally confirmed by later historians, it is clear that the German freemen, though far from being the squalid savages that they have been sometimes represented, were not industrious tillers of the soil.   War, the chase, the sword-dance, and the throw of the dice-box were their chief excitements, and when they were not excited they were torpid and lethargic.   Long and heavy potations, sometimes continued for a day and night together, sometimes interrupted by a bloody brawl, were followed by equally long and heavy slumbers.   Whether they went to the banquet or to market they always wore arms, a sure sign of a low state of civilisation ; and the gravest affairs were all discussed amid copious draughts of beer, or, if the disputants dwelt near the Rhine or the Danube, of wine from the land of the Romans.   In short, while we can trace in the Teuton of the first Christian centuries some noble qualities—truth, courage, chastity—we also discover the marks of some deep inbred vices, which beset him till this day, especially drunkenness and the love of gambling ; and we do *not* find even the germs of that capacity for steady and continuous toil which, since they became Christian and civilised, has been the glory of the German, the Anglo-Saxon, and the Scandinavian.

Such, then, in brief outline, seems to have been the ordinary life of a German village.   The political institutions of the Teutonic races—which are what we are chiefly now concerned with—depended on the manner and extent of the consolidation of these

How the village community developed into the state.

villages into larger and more powerful communities. If we go up to some high table-land we shall see little brooks and streams running off from it in all directions, some of which will perhaps eventually form part of a great and world-famous river, while others will find their way unnoticed to the sea. In studying the early history of the Germanic tribes, we stand on such a table-land. The future fortunes of Franks, Visigoths, Burgundians, Angles, Saxons, are involved in the village politics of these much-drinking, freely-fighting German boors; but there are also involved the obscure destinies of countless little tribes, whose uncouth names survive only in the pages of Tacitus or Jordanes, and are in fact forgotten by men.

Manifold-ness of German political life.

The characteristic of German polity, as much in the first century after Christ as in the sixteenth, as much in the time of Arminius as in that of Charles V, was its infinite diversity. There were tribes that knew no king, tribes that had kings with very limited powers, tribes that submitted to despotism—or something very like it—on the part of their kings, and tribes that even endured to have such authority over them exercised by a woman. And the chief—I will not say the only—cause of this diversity seems to have been the relative greatness or littleness of the clusters into which the village communities ultimately coalesced; and, closely connected herewith, the question whether the organism which was thus finally formed entertained widely extended schemes of aggression and foreign conquest, or whether it rested

content with the defence of its own narrow borders
against an invading foe.

Apparently every German village, at the time which *The Pagus,*
we are now considering, had so far coalesced with *Gau,*
County or
some of its neighbours as to form what the Romans *Canton.*
called a *pagus*. The extent of these *pagi*, and the
number of *vici* which united to form them, doubtless
differed exceedingly, but as we find that in the time
of Caesar [1] each Suevic *pagus* sent forth 1000 armed
men, an equal number remaining at home to till the
ground, we may perhaps assume that the whole
population of a *pagus* generally consisted of about
10,000 persons, and that about ten *vici*, more or less,
contributed to its formation. The choice of a Teutonic word to represent the term *pagus*, which,
though convenient, is foreign, has not been found
easy. Modern German scholars have generally
adopted the word *Gau*, which was extensively used
in the Middle Ages, though it is admitted that this
does not precisely correspond to the *pagus*, but was
often of somewhat smaller extent. As an English
equivalent, *county* or *shire* comes the nearest, though
both of them suggest ideas of a somewhat later time[2].
Whether such a translation be scientifically accurate
or not[3] there can be little doubt that the feeling of

[1] De Bello Gallico iv. 1.

[2] We have a word *Gá* in English akin to the German *Gau*, but
it does not seem to have been ever extensively used. For the
reasons why *shire* is not precisely appropriate, see Prof. Freeman's
Essay ' The Shire and the Gá.' Have we a trace of the Gau in the
names of Linlithgow and Glasgow ?

[3] Bishop Stubbs makes the ' hundred' answer to the *pagus*, but as

local patriotism which still animates a Devonshire man or a Shropshire man when he speaks of his county, represents, at least as well as any other modern equivalent, the bond which bound a German warrior to his *pagus*. But, upon the whole, the Swiss *canton*, both in extent and in the manner of its growth, namely, by the coalition of the inhabitants of several neighbouring valleys, seems to me the most fitting representative of the *pagus* of the *Germania*.

Some German communities, perhaps, stopped in the process of consolidation at the canton, and never reached a further stage. They may have had traditions, and even religious rites, which kept alive the remembrance that they formed part of a larger tribe, that they were Suevi, or Mattiaci, or Chauci ; but as far as political organisation went they were willing to be a *pagus* and nothing more. If so, we may probably affirm that the tribes which contained many of these self-isolated cantons retained what has been called their 'republican' organisation, engaged but little in offensive war, were feeble in their resistance to Rome, and have left but little mark in history.

Several Pagi might coalesce into a Civitas. The first step towards national existence on a larger scale was taken when many *pagi*, bound together for the most part by the traditions of a common origin, organised themselves into what the Romans called a *civitas*, and in doing so generally, perhaps not always, elected for themselves a King. I do not think it is possible to find a term which

there were 65 hundreds in Sussex alone, this seems a very small division to represent the great and important *pagi* of Caesar and Tacitus.

exactly represents the stage of development which
was thus reached, but the Saxon and Anglian kingdoms which were set up in our own land—Wessex,
Mercia, Northumbria—will convey the true idea of
it to our minds better than an elaborate description.

Kingship and a tendency towards unification went *Kingship*
hand in hand in the history of the German races. *and*
And not in that history alone: we may safely *tendency*
towards
illustrate the tendency of the kingly office among *unification*
the Germans by what we read in the Old Testament *went to-*
gether.
of the election of Saul.   The Twelve Tribes of
Israel, conscious that they were losing national
unity and were in danger of being absorbed by the
great monarchies on their borders, elected Saul to
be their king, and his very first act of kingship
was the deliverance of the outlying settlement of
Jabesh-gilead from the destruction with which it was
threatened by Nahash, King of the Ammonites.   In
our own days we have seen the aspirations of the
Germans after national unity, aspirations which
seemed for centuries doomed to hopeless failure,
at length successful; and the visible token of their
success and of that victory over their foes which unity
made possible, was the crowning of the Emperor
William by a host of kings, dukes and generals[1],
in the palace of Versailles.   We must not press the
conclusion too far, since the history both of Rome and
of the United States of America shows that a Republic
can found a great dominion and defend the oneness

[1] Compare the 'Turba regum diversarumque nationum ductores'
of Jordanes, De Reb. Get. xxxviii.

of a nation: but for the German peoples, properly
so called, I think we may safely say Monarchy has
meant Unity, and Unity has meant Monarchy.

*Character
of the
kingly office
among the
Germans.*

Far other, however, than the languid despot upon
the sanctity of whose presence-chamber we intruded
in the beginning of this lecture, was the King of the
Goths or the Alamanni. Whether himself the son
of a king or not, it was necessary that he should be
of noble birth[1], and he had therefore probably been
reared in a house, rude but somewhat larger than
the ordinary freeman's dwelling, built by the side of
a fountain or near a sacred grove, at some little
distance from the village settlement[2]. But his life had
been passed in the active exercises of war and the
chase: and before he was chosen king of a great and
important *civitas* he had probably given some proof
of valour and ability, to cause him to be singled out
from the ranks of nobles, each of whom was a chief
in his own canton. Even after his election as king,
his power was by no means unlimited. He might
not bind nor strike any one of the free German
warriors under him. Both in council and in war he
had so much authority as his gifts of intellect, of
daring, or of strength enabled him to acquire and

[1] 'Reges ex nobilitate, duces ex virtute sumunt' (Tacitus, Germania vii).

[2] 'Colunt discreti ac diversi, ut fons, ut campus, ut nemus placuit' (ibid. xvi). It seems very likely, as suggested by Seebohm (English Village Community, p. 339), that this describes rather the settlement of the chiefs than of the commonalty. This must be stated, however, as a mere conjecture, as there is nothing in the language of Tacitus on which to found it.

retain, and not much more[1]. And when thus elected
he had no absolute right to transmit his crown to his
first-born, nor indeed to any of his sons. Doubtless
the eldest son of a recently deceased king, if himself
a man of capacity and valour, had always a good
chance of being chosen to succeed him, but that was
all. Gradually as the nation and its royal race grew
accustomed to one another, and especially when the
kings of that race had often led the nation to victory,

[1] The story of Clovis and the vase of Soissons, though almost
worn threadbare by frequent repetition, may be quoted as an illustration of the nature of the power of a German king, strictly limited
in peace, but tending to become absolute in war. Clovis wished to
gratify the Bishop of Rheims by restoring to him a vase which the
spoilers had taken from his church. When the army were all
mustered at Soissons with the heap of plunder before them, he
accordingly asked that this vase might be allotted to him over and
above his regular share of the spoil. 'Glorious king,' said the
loyal soldiers, 'we and all that we have are thine, neither can any
one resist thy power.' But one of the warriors—'envious and fickle,'
says the historian, perhaps in his heart resenting the adulation of
his comrades—lifted up his battle-axe and smote upon the vase,
saying, 'Nothing shalt thou carry away from hence except what
a fair lot give thee.' The vase was apparently defaced, not broken,
and the king concealing his annoyance handed it to the bishop's
messenger. At the year's end, when all the warriors were assembled
in the Campus Martius to show the brightness of their arms, the
king, going the round of his troops, came to the striker of the vase.
'No one,' said he, 'keeps his arms in such a dirty state as thou
dost : neither thy spear, nor thy shield, nor thy battle-axe is fit to be
seen,' and therewith he wrested the battle-axe from his hand and
threw it to the ground. As the man stooped to pick it up the king
raised his hand on high, and drove his own battle-axe deep into the
warrior's skull, shouting, 'Thus at Soissons didst thou do to that
vase.' Thereupon he ordered all the other warriors to file off from
the field, their hearts being filled with a salutary dread of his power.

the feeling grew stronger and stronger that out of
that race only the nation ought to choose its kings.
Thus were the Amals looked upon as the natural
kingly race of the Ostrogoths, the Merwings of the
Franks, the Asdings of the Vandals. But still there
was no strict hereditary right, and the nation on the
death of its king exercised its power of choice often
in utter defiance of the rule of primogeniture.

Meeting of the members of the Civitas.　　The choice of the ruler, the decision as to war
or peace, the enactment of a few very simple laws,
these formed the chief business of the assembly of
the *civitas*, which was called probably by some name
like our own Anglo-Saxon Folc-gemot or Folcs-
thing. Tacitus gives us a concise but vivid picture
of the proceedings of one of these national assemblies. The *gemots-men* indicated their deep-
seated love of liberty by the unpunctuality of their
attendance. Two days, and sometimes three, would
elapse before a sufficient number had arrived to
enable them to commence their proceedings. Then,
when the crowd was in the humour for beginning,
they sat down on the ground, all arrayed in their
armour. The priests called for silence, and upon
them rested the duty of maintaining order during
the deliberations of the assembly[1]. Then the king

[1] In this connection it is interesting to note that an inscription
has recently been discovered at the Roman Camp of Borcovicus
in Northumberland, which commences ' Deo Marti Thincso.' The
persons who thus record the dedication of their altar to the god
Mars Thincsus are said to be ' Germani Cives Tuihanti.' Dr.
Hübner, one of the greatest authorities on Roman epigraphy, believes
that ' Mars Thincsus ' is the Teutonic god Tiu, and that his epithet

or chief whose age, or eloquence, or noble birth gave him the right of pre-audience, addressed the assembly, and afterwards each in his turn according to the same blended qualifications. All the speakers sought rather to persuade than to command. An unpopular proposal was drowned in murmurs of disapproval, while eagerly brandished lances testified the applause and the agreement of the assembly.

In these assemblies an accusation might be brought *Judicial* against a man who was suspected of treason against *power of the popular* the nation's life, and if the charge were pushed home, *assembly.* a capital sentence was pronounced upon the offender. Betrayers and deserters were hanged from a tree ; the mere coward and fugitive, the man whom our Saxon forefathers would have called a *nithing*, was plunged deep in mud and covered with a hurdle to prevent his struggling back to life—a mode of punishment which reminds one of some scenes in Dante's *Inferno*.

Probably, however, it was neither the legislative *Election of the King.* nor the judicial, but the elective aspect of these national councils which was the most important. The chiefs, or elders, or judges, or by whatever name they were called, the men whose business it was to administer a rude justice in the cantons and the villages, were chosen in the national council[1].

means that the national *Thing* or Council was held under his guardianship. (See Archaeologia Aeliana, x. 154–159.)

[1] 'Eliguntur in iisdem conciliis et principes, qui jura per pagos vicosque reddunt' (Tacitus, Germania xii).

And the highest act of the nation's great assize was performed when the chief who was to repel the eagles of Rome, to lead the people across the frozen Danube, or to swoop upon the wealthy plains of Gaul, was solemnly chosen king. The clashing arms testified the nation's assent to his nomination. Six strong warriors slowly upheaved the shield on which stood the newly-chosen one, and shouts of 'Thiudans! Thiudans[1]!' proclaimed to the echoing hills that the nation had once more a king. Thus was he singled out from his fellows who was to conduct the people's quarrel with the far-off, mysterious, Imperator of Rome.

[1] Thiudans is the Gothic word for ' King.'

LECTURE III.

THE COMING OF THE HUNS.

HAVING thus given a cursory glance at the political and social condition of the Roman Empire and its German neighbours in the fourth century after Christ, let us now even more briefly survey the ethnological aspect of the barbarian world on its northern frontier at the same time.

Of the three great groups into which the non-Latin nations of Europe are at this day divided, Celtic, Teutonic, and Slavonic, the Teutonic alone here claims our especial attention. The Celtic nationality had been beaten down in ten years of battle by Julius Caesar, and its last hope of offering a successful resistance to Rome vanished when Suetonius Paulinus crossed the straits of Menai and put the Druids to the sword in their hitherto inviolable island of Mona. The Slavonic group of nations, which now fills Russia and Poland, forms half the population of Austria and is founding new kingdoms and principalities in what was lately Turkey in Europe, had not then come fully on the stage of history. The vague term Sarmatians, used by Roman geographers, is probably the best indication that we have of their presence in Europe, but few ethnological questions are harder than to define the ever-shifting boundary which separated them from their Teutonic neighbours. It is very possible that many of the barbarian hosts that warred on Rome may have consisted of Slavonic marauders led on by Teutonic chieftains: but just because the initiative at any rate belonged to the Teutons, and because the Slaves originated so few expeditions against the Empire, we may practically leave them out of the question and consider only the great Teutonic population which, all round the northern frontier of the Empire, from the mouth of the Rhine to the mouth of the Danube, faced the Masters of the Soldiery and their Legions.

Tendency of the Teutonic nations to form confederacies.
There had been a marked tendency during the third century after Christ in the barbarian nations to merge themselves into a few great confederacies, a tendency which possibly had something to do with the ill-success of the Roman arms during that period. A whole string of names of petty tribes on the lower Rhine, mentioned to us by Tacitus, disappears in order to form the nation of the *Franks*. In like manner the tribes which dwelt on the Main and the Neckar clustered together into the confederation of the *Alamanni*. On the Middle Danube the great nation of the Marcomanni, who once pressed Marcus Aurelius hard, disappeared, and no one nation of pre-eminent power arose in its place; but when we come towards the mouth of the Danube, to the countries which are now known as Roumania, Tran-

Franks.

Alamanni.

sylvania, and Bessarabia, we find them occupied by the great and powerful confederacy of the *Goths.* *Goths.* This race, of pure Teutonic origin, belonging to that which is called the Low-German family of peoples, and speaking a language much more akin to Lowland Scotch than to the modern German of Hanover, had migrated, probably in the second century of our era, from the district now known as East Prussia in the south-east corner of the Baltic. They had spread themselves along the northern shore of the Euxine, near the mouths of the Dnieper and the Dniester, and after a series of piratical expeditions by sea and marauding inroads by land upon the Eastern half of the Empire, had occupied without further opposition the Roman province of Dacia, constituted by Trajan in the early part of the second century. During the century before our narrative begins, they had been dwelling for the most part as friendly and peaceable neighbours of Rome. They had become gradually divided into two great groups of peoples, the Eastern and Western Goths, who eventually became known as the Ostrogoths and Visigoths.

A hard and undeserved fate, as well as an un- *Associa-* merited glory, has come upon the possessors of the *tions con-* *nected with* Gothic name. The glory is that of having given *the term* their name to the most solemn and impressive order *Gothic.* of architecture that the world has ever seen. Men speak, and doubtless will ever continue to speak, of Gothic buildings, though the last traces of Gothic nationality had expired many centuries before a pointed arch was seen at Canterbury or Notre Dame.

On the other hand the expression 'What a Goth!'
as indicative of rudeness and lack of culture, is constantly used by the descendants of men who were
centuries behind the Goths in refinement and civilisation, and who do not know that 'What a Frank!'
or 'What a Saxon!' would be far nearer to historic
truth.　In point of fact, of all the Teutonic races
none showed so early an appreciation of what was
best in Roman civilisation as the Gothic, none
showed a greater power of assimilating that civilisation, and none, had its career not been prematurely
cut short, would more happily for Europe have
blended the old with the new by uniting the culture
and refinement of 'Romania' with the rough energy
and freedom of 'Barbaricum.'

*The Visi-
goths and
the Empire.*　At the particular period which we have reached
these remarks apply rather to the Visigoth than to
the Ostrogoth.　While the Ostrogoths, wandering
wide over the vast plains of Southern Russia, were
coming in contact with and subduing the dim Slavonic peoples of the interior, and thus building up
*Circa
350–376.*　for their great king, Hermanric, a vast but ill-con-
solidated empire which his flatterers—those of them
at least who had some slight knowledge of classical
history—compared to that of Alexander the Great,
the Visigoths dwelling in Transylvania and Walla-
chia, and acknowledging perhaps in a general way
the suzerainty of Hermanric, but under the especial
rule of their own native chieftains who bore the
subordinate title of *Judges*, were continually coming
more and more under the influence of the Empire.

Latin and Greek words were creeping into their language. The soldier talked of his pay as *mizdo* (evidently the same word as the Greek μισθός), and of his rations as *anno* (probably the Latin *annona*). The *alewa* displayed to the grateful husbandman the fatness of the olive-tree, and he carried home its produce in a *sakkus.*

Not only words like these and a knowledge of the arts of civilised life, but more far-reaching thoughts, those which overleap the grave and bind together in one all the generations of the family of God, were vibrating through the Visigothic brain. Ulfilas, the great Apostle of the Goths, himself a Goth, but resident in early manhood at Constantinople, began his missionary career in 341, and continued it for forty years, labouring during all that time by his tongue and pen at the conversion of his countrymen to Christianity. As an instrument in this great work he translated the Bible into Gothic, only omitting, according to the well-known story, the books of Samuel and Kings, 'inasmuch as they contain the story of the wars, and the Gothic race was already fond enough of war, and needed rather a bit to hold it back from battle, than any spur to urge it thereunto.' This Gothic Bible is a priceless possession for the philologist, being by far the earliest monument of any Teutonic language, and illustrating in a countless variety of ways, both the distant relationship which connects our family of languages with Sanskrit, Greek, and Latin, and the points at which the members of our own family, German, Danish,

Ulfilas and the Gothic Bible.

348-370. Dutch, English, have parted company one from another.

Persecution of Gothic Christians.   The success of Ulfilas in Christianising the Goths was so great that a persecution arose, under the stress of which many of his converts determined to leave their homes and seek shelter in the dominions of the great Christian Emperor. This happened about the year 348. The emigrants, with Ulfilas at their head, 'a second Moses,' as he was often styled by his contemporaries, crossed the Danube and founded a settlement in the country about Nicopolis, on the northern slopes of the Balkans. Here their descendants were still living after the lapse of nearly two centuries[1], being known by the name of the Lesser Goths, 'a numerous people, but poor and unwarlike, having no abundance of anything, save cattle of divers kinds, sheep and pastures and forests ; having no wheat, though the soil is fertile in other crops. Vineyards they do not possess, but some of them as merchants buy wine from the neighbouring district : but most of them are nourished on milk.'

Probably Ulfilas did not remain constantly with his Lesser Goths in Moesia, but often crossed the Danube into Dacia, to strengthen the faith of his remaining converts there, or to add to their number. Apparently a second persecution broke out (if, indeed, it had ever ceased to rage) about 370. From a fragment of a Gothic calendar we learn that the 23rd October was dedicated 'to the remembrance of

[1] In 552, see Jordanes lii.

many martyrs among the Gothic people, and of 370-375.
Frederic' (doubtless one of the heroes of the perse-
cution), and that the 29th was similarly dedicated 'to
the remembrance of the martyrs who remained, with
Priest Vereka and Batvin, members of the Catholic
Church, and were burned among the Gothic people.'

The leader of the persecuting party at this time *Athanaric* was Judge Athanaric, a stern, unbending Gothic *Judge of the Visigoths.* chief, who would brook no compromise with Rome
or Roman ways, who had sworn a terrible oath that
he would never set foot on Roman soil, and who
now, to the cruel utmost of his power, strove to prevent Odin and Thunnor from being driven out of
the Home of Gods by the Nazarene, whose cross
glittered upon the banners of Rome.

On the opposite side, as leader of that section of *Fritigern.*
the Visigoths which favoured the Roman civilisation
and the Christian religion, appears the gallant Fritigern, one of the most attractive figures whom Gothic
history presents to us.   The contention between
him and the bigoted old Gothic party under Athanaric was so sharp that it seems to have broken out
into actual war, in which, as one author [1] tells us,
Fritigern, on formally announcing his conversion to
Christianity, asked and received the help of the
Roman Emperor against his rival.

Such, then, was the relation of 'Barbaricum' *Outlook in* towards 'Romania' about the year 375. Reading (as *375.* we are too apt to do) our knowledge of subsequent
events into the history of that year, when the fourth

[1] Socrates, iv. 33.

375. century of our era had reached its fourth quarter, it is
easy to imagine the Roman Empire lying rich and de-
fenceless, at the mercy of barbarian foes all round its
border and all athirst to devour it.   But such was certainly not the aspect which it then wore to its contemporaries.   The keen eye of a statesman, if he were
also possessed of fine ethical instincts, might undoubtedly perceive many dangerous symptoms of
moral and spiritual decay, from which he might
forebode its future downfall ; but to the ordinary
observer, especially to the ordinary barbarian observer, seldom had the great fabric of Roman civilisation seemed stronger or more imposing.   Of anything
like a combined attack of the barbarian hordes upon
the Roman frontier, no barbarian dreamed.   A petty
raid here or there might perhaps be successfully
executed, and might enable its perpetrator to return
with some cattle from a few Moesian farms, or some
bracelets and golden chains from a sacked Illyrian
town.   But this was the height of his ambition as
Rome's enemy.   He would much rather be Rome's
friend : enter her service as a leader of *foederati*[1] ;
mount guard in the ante-chamber of the Emperor ;
direct the arms of Rome against some hated rival
chief ; perhaps, even—supreme felicity—attain in
his well-fed and corpulent old age to the overwhelming honour of a Roman consulship.

Sudden ap-   The appearance on the northern shore of the Sea
pearance of of Azof of a horde of squalid savages from the steppes
the Huns.

[1] Gothic Irregulars.

of Central Asia, each riding a little pony as ugly and 374.
as unkempt as himself, changed the whole current of
men's thoughts, and was the first visible link in the
chain which drew mediaeval Europe, the Europe of
Charlemagne, Barbarossa, and Dante,

' forth from the abyss of things that were to be.'

These savages were the terrible Huns, of whose
history I shall have to speak somewhat more in
detail in my sixth lecture. For the present it will
be enough to quote a chapter from the work of the
Gothic historian Jordanes, in order to show how the
Asiatic intruders were looked upon by the first European nation with whom they came in contact[1].

'After no great interval of time the nations of the *Descrip-*
Huns, more cruel than Ferocity itself, flamed forth *tion of the*
against the Goths. An unhallowed union between *Huns by*
unclean spirits wandering through the wilderness, *Jordanes.*
and certain Gothic women expelled [centuries before]
for witchcraft from the tents of their countrymen,
gave birth to this most ferocious people, which dwelt
at first among the marshes—small, foul, and skinny,
hardly human, but spoken of as men because they
possessed something which distantly resembled human speech. This wild race formerly dwelt on the
further shore of the Sea of Azof, and there practised
no other labour than hunting, except that after they
had grown into a great people they harried the neighbouring nations with constant robberies and frauds.
Now when the huntsmen of this people were, according to their custom, pursuing the chase on the

[1] Jordanes, De Rebus Geticis xxiv.

further shore of Azof, behold, upon a sudden, a female stag presented herself to their view, and stepping into the pool, first going forth and then stopping, seemed to offer herself as guide of their journey. Following her lead, therefore, the huntsmen passed over on foot through the Sea of Azof, which they had before thought to be as impassable as the ocean. Soon, too, when the Gothic shore loomed up before those unknown visitors, the stag disappeared. This, I trow, was done by those spirits to whom the Huns owed their origin, in order to spite the Gothic people. The huntsmen who had before thought that there was no other world beyond the Sea of Azof, were stricken with admiration of the Gothic land, the road to which, hitherto unknown, they deemed had been shown to them by the gods, and going back to their own people, persuaded them to hasten by the path which the stag had pointed out to them into the territory of the Goths. All whom they met on the way fell victims to their fury, and as soon as they had crossed that vast pool, five nations [whose uncouth names I need not transcribe] were swept away by that whirlwind of savage tribes. The Alans also, who were a match for them in war, but very unlike them in civilisation, in appearance, and in diet, were wearied out by them in incessant fighting, and at length subdued. For those whom they would perhaps never have conquered in fair fight they put to flight by the terribleness of their appearance, throwing the utmost possible hideousness into the expression of their faces, which were naturally of

a frightful blackness, and resembled, if I may say so, 374.
a shapeless lump of dough rather than a face, having
two black points in them instead of eyes. This
scowling countenance reveals the boldness [? cru-
elty] of their hearts, who rage against their new-
born offspring even on the first day of their birth,
for all the male children's cheeks are gashed by them
with an iron tool, in order that before they begin to
receive the nourishment of their mother's milk they
may learn to bear the pain of a wound. Hence
their youth lacks the beauty, and their old age the
dignity of a beard, because their faces, furrowed with
iron, lose through scars the seasonable beauty of
hair. They are little in stature, but nimble and clever
in their movements, and especially ready in horse-
manship : with broad shoulders, arms well adapted
to the use of the bow, necks strong, and heads
always held erect with pride. In short these people,
wearing the shape of man, practise in their lives the
ferocity of beasts.'

Through the uncouth sentences of the half-
educated Gothic historian the general character of
the Hunnish invaders may be sufficiently discerned.
They stood on a distinctly lower grade of civilisation
than any of the Teutonic invaders of the Empire.
The Goth, the Frank, the Alaman, the Vandal
were barbarians indeed, but barbarians with some
capacity—in the case of the Goth with an extraordinary capacity—for appreciating the advantages
of civilisation. The Hun, fresh from his centuries of

wandering over the high table-land of Tartary, was an utter, an irreclaimable savage. To compare them with some of the native races with which our own has recently come in contact, the Goth was like the Maori, the Hun like a stronger and more warlike Australian savage.

The Huns were ' Turanians,' not Aryans.

This social difference between the Hun and the Teuton corresponds to a deep ethnological chasm. Hitherto all the great struggles in which the European nations had been engaged (except the Punic wars) had been waged between members of the great Aryan family of nations. Persian, Greek, Italian, Celt, Teuton, however wide their divergences of religion, of culture, of intellectual development, were yet all children of the same family, some of whom, so to speak, had come of age, and entered into their inheritance, while others were still in a state of infancy and untaught childhood. But the Hun had no such link with the great historic peoples of the Mediterranean Sea. In his language probably no germ of affinity with Greek or Sanskrit would have been discernible. Wheresoever the common home of the Indo-European peoples may eventually be located, it is certain that the progenitors of the Hun never dwelt there. He was of kin to the Mongol, the Calmuck, the Turk, not to the Roman or the Englishman. In the world's history he stands in line with Jenghiz Khan, with Tamerlane, with Bajazet, not with Alexander or with Caesar. In one word— to adopt a term which, however inaccurate, is convenient—he was not Aryan, but Turanian.

Such then were the invaders from Asia, who, about *374.* the year 374, precipitated themselves upon the settle- *A nation of light* ments of the Ostrogoths in Southern Russia.   What *cavalry.* they may have lacked in size they made up in nimble- ness of movement, and against the Goths, who do not appear to have been pre-eminently an equestrian people, they had this advantage, that every man of the tribe was mounted, and mounted on a hardy wiry little steed, which was probably satisfied with the roughest food, and which so perfectly understood its rider's wishes, that it seemed as if horse and horseman were one being.

Details as to the conflict between the Huns and *Hermanric* the Ostrogoths are utterly wanting, but it is clear *defeated.* that the latter were completely defeated. Hermanric, 'the Ostrogothic Alexander' who is said to have reached the age of 110, in his rage and shame put an end to his own life. His wide but loosely compacted empire was broken up.   Some Ostrogoths, under a prince of the house of Hermanric, moved south- wards, and took part in the events which we are about to notice, on the Danube.   But the larger part of the nation submitted to inevitable necessity and bowed their necks to the yoke.   For three quarters of a century the Ostrogoths formed part of the great Hunnish Empire, and their sovereigns, descendants of the great Hermanric, ruled as vassals of the Hunnish king.

The barbarian flood rolled on and reached the *Athanaric* river Dniester and the long line of earthworks *defeated.* which apparently separated the land of the Visigoths

375.   from that of the Ostrogoths [1].   Here Athanaric had
drawn up his men, expecting a regular attack, to
which he would have been prepared with a regular
reply.   Little did he know the nature of the nimble
savages with whom he had to deal.   Having learned
from their scouts where the bulk of the Visigothic
army was posted (which was probably by the rampart
rather than by the river), and having found a ford
across the Dniester, they crossed that ford by moon-
light and fell like a thunderbolt on the flank of the
unsuspecting Athanaric.   He was stupefied at the
assault, he saw his bravest friends slain, and he
found he had no resource but flight.   Withdrawing
to the Carpathians he began to construct a new line
of defence, partly formed by those mountains and
partly by the river Sereth.   He would have had but
little leisure to construct this new stronghold, had
not the Huns been so burdened with their booty
that they could not follow him in haste.

The Visi-
goths seek
refuge
within the
Empire.
        And now that the strongest Gothic champions had
been worsted, dismay and despair entered the hearts
of the Visigoths.   To share the hardships of a life
in the Carpathians with Athanaric was not the course
which commended itself to the majority.   They looked
across the broad Danube to the well-tilled plains of
Moesia ; they thought of the tightening bond which
had of late united them to the Empire ; they turned
to Fritigern, the steadfast partisan of Rome, and
deemed that through his friendship for the Emperor

---

[1] ' Vallis Greuthungorum ' (Ammianus xxxi. 3).   Greuthungi
seems to have been another name for the Ostrogoths.

they might find a refuge from the storm.   Fritigern 376.
(who, with a perhaps older colleague, Alavivus, is
always spoken of as leader of the migration) may
perhaps, through Ulfilas, have opened negotiations
with the Imperial Court, negotiations which occupied
many weeks, for Valens, the reigning Emperor, was
at Antioch.   The terms which Fritigern offered were
that the Goths would all enter the military service
of the Empire, and apparently that those who were
still heathens would embrace the Emperor's creed,
which was one of the many forms of Arian Christianity.
On the other hand there must have been some stipu-
lation as to the supply of food, at least for one season,
to give the new-comers time to till the fields for a
future harvest.

While the tedious negotiations were going forward, *The Goths*
a strange sight might be seen on that Wallachian *on the shore of the*
shore of the Danube, where Europe beheld, in 1877, *Danube.*
the vast host of the Russians manœuvring backwards
and forwards, in order to find a place where they
might cross into Bulgaria.   On that same shore in
the autumn of 376 stood 200,000 Goths, stretching
out their hands in the attitude of entreaty, bewailing
the hard fate that had befallen them, and shouting
out, whenever a Roman official came within hearing,
their eager offers of fealty to the Emperor.

At length the answer came from Antioch.   Valens *Valens*
was flattered by the prospect of the submission of so *gives them permission*
many stalwart warriors ; he persuaded himself that *to cross.*
by enlisting them under his standards he might
lighten the pressure of taxation on his subjects ; he

perhaps also thought that in the battle of the creeds which was still being waged, the adhesion of a strong and warlike nation to his own Arian form of faith would secure for it the victory. This last consideration, however, which is all-important on the pages of the ecclesiastical historians, was probably only a secondary one in the minds of the Emperor and his Council.

The Danube crossed.

Whatever the determining cause may have been, the Imperial orders came to Lupicinus the Count of Thrace, and Maximus the Duke of Moesia, that the refugees were to be admitted into the Empire on condition that they gave up their arms, and that the boys who were still under age for martial service should be surrendered as hostages to be quartered in various distant cities of the Empire. Thus the long suspense was ended. The Visigoths, who night after night had feared to see the Hunnish watch-fires blazing in the north and to hear the discordant battle-cry of the Asiatics sounding in their ears, were relieved from their terrible anxiety. To have to part with their gallant sons was hard : to have to part with their old and trusty broadswords was harder, but life was sweet. There was the Moesian shore and safety under the shadow of Rome, and here were the sloops ready to carry them across to the Promised Land. Night and day, for several days, the sloops were crossing and re-crossing, till at length 200,000 Gothic warriors, with their wives, and children, and aged parents, stood on the soil of the Empire. They stood there, not unarmed.

Already they had made their first experience of the
gigantic corruption of the Imperial service. Lupicinus and Maximus, and the officers under them,
avaricious and lustful men, while superintending the
transport of the Goths, were thinking all the time
how to fill their villas with precious spoil and beautiful captives, rather than how to obey the orders
of the Emperor. While they were intent on the
golden torques, the linen robes, the costly-fringed
carpets of the Goths, they allowed the broadswords
and the hunting-knives to pass unquestioned. Already before the disembarkation was well over, a
bitter sense of wrong, and consciousness of power
to avenge that wrong, were brooding in thousands
of Gothic hearts.

*376.
Rapacity of
the Roman
officials.*

We may perhaps say of the reception by Valens
of the Gothic fugitives, as of Elizabeth's reception of
Mary Queen of Scots, that either the request for
asylum should have been refused, or, if granted, it
should have been granted generously. There was
abundance of room doubtless in the solitary spaces
of Moesia for 200,000 sturdy cultivators, and if they
had been wisely and fairly treated they might have
formed a stout barrier against all other barbarian
invaders. Who can say? The Roman Empire
might be standing yet.

‘ Trojaque nunc staret, Priamique arx alta maneret.’

But now, in addition to the grievance of their treasures stolen, came the far sorer grievance of food
withheld. The promised rations, perhaps partly
from incompetence as well as from bad faith, were

376. not forthcoming. With such money as they still possessed the unhappy Goths offered to buy food: Lupicinus and Maximus bought up dogs from all the districts round and sold their flesh to the starving immigrants in return for slaves, among whom were some of the sons of the noblest of the Goths, driven to barter even their children for life. Such wickedness as this, thank God, does not often miss its reward even in this world.

A few months, however, elapsed before the storm of vengeance burst forth. Let us take advantage of that short interval to describe the characters of the rulers of the Roman State.

Roman Emperors.

West, Valentinian I, 364–375.

For eleven years (364–375) after the death of Julian 'the Apostate' and his short-lived successor Jovian, Valentinian's strong hand was at the Empire's helm. A blunt, untutored soldier, with a strange dash of cruelty in his nature, he was nevertheless a good ruler for those times. He held an even bálance between the warring Christian sects, insisting on toleration all round; he was careful not to oppress his subjects by too heavy taxation; he defended them from the barbarians, and he repressed the licentiousness which was sapping the energies of the Empire. The worst thing that he did for his country was associating his brother Valens in the throne, giving him the rule over the East. Both in person and character Valens presented a striking contrast to his brother. Valentinian was strong and well-shaped, with a bright complexion and clear blue eye: everything about him told of energy and de-

East, Valens, 364–378.

cision. Valens, torpid and procrastinating, with 376.
muddy complexion, lack-lustre eye, bent legs and
protuberant belly, neither looked nor spoke like an
Emperor of Rome. And over against Valentinian's
inflexible and universal religious tolerance had to be
set the somewhat bitter Arianism of Valens.

A year before the Hunnish irruption into Europe *West,*
Valentinian died, leaving his brother Valens Em- *Gratian,*
peror of the East, and his two sons, Gratian and *375–383.*
Valentinian II, Emperors of the West, the former *nian II,*
at Trier, the latter at Milan. Gratian was a lad full *375–392.*
of noble promise, but only sixteen years of age ;
Valentinian II was a child of four, under the regency of his mother, Justina. Decidedly the Imperial partnership was weak, ill-adapted for the
strain of a great crisis, and what made it get weaker
was that it was not united. The dull soul of the
sluggish Valens was jealous of his brilliant nephew,
who was already showing military aptitudes and
earning the devotion of his troops. Justina also,
who was the second wife of the deceased Emperor,
looked probably with no friendly eye on the growing
reputation of her step-son. The *Concordia Augus-*
torum[1], which was so often celebrated on the Imperial medals, was not strong in the year 376.

We return to the affairs of the betrayed and *The ban-*
hunger-stricken Goths. There was as yet no open *quet at*
insurrection, but Alavivus and Fritigern were march- *Marcian-*
ing about in Moesia in a way which seemed to in- *ople.*

[1] Concord Auggg. (The number of repetitions of the letter *g*
indicates the number of Emperors.)

377. dicate independence· and growing suspicion ; and, moreover, some of the bands of their Ostrogothic cousins had taken advantage of the disorder of the times, and the occupied attention of the Imperial soldiery, to cross the Danube on rafts and pitch their camp not far from Fritigern's. Before long Alavivus and Fritigern appeared at the gates of Marcianople (the modern Shumla), an important city at the intersection of two great cross-roads, and commanding a pass through the Balkans. The two Visigothic chiefs were still ostensibly captains of the Emperor's *foederati,* and Lupicinus, Count of Thrace, bade them to a banquet. The barbarians who followed them had flocked into the city to purchase provisions. A dispute arose between them and the citizens which led to bloodshed, and the news of the disturbance reached Lupicinus when he was reclining at the luxurious banquet, flushed with wine and scarcely keeping his heavy eyes open by gazing at the performers of a pantomime. Languidly he ordered the tall young Gothic nobles who were keeping guard over their chief at the door of the *praetorium* to be hewn down by the far more numerous Roman soldiery. The groans of the dying, and the battle-shout of those who were yet fighting for their lives, penetrated the innermost chambers of the palace, and aroused Fritigern from the pleasures of the dainty repast. If his host sought to soothe him by alleging that it was only a drunken brawl that was going on outside,

'his soul more truly knew that sound too well.'

He drew his sword and stalked down through the 377.
banquet hall, exclaiming that if there was a tumult
among the Goths he alone could quell it.   The
pretext, or the naked sword, secured him a safe
passage through the trembling ranks of the banqueters.   He was received with a shout of joy by
his surviving companions.   They mounted their
horses and rode out of the gates of the city; and
now, openly declaring war against the Empire, began
to plunder and to burn the rich farmsteads in the
neighbourhood of Marcianople.   Lupicinus marched
forth to meet them at the ninth milestone from the
city; but his troops, hastily collected, were badly
led.   The Goths, in their fury and despair, beat
down their enemies.   All the tribunes (commissioned
officers) and the larger part of the rank and file were
stretched in death upon the plain.   The base Lupicinus, whose cruelty and avarice had caused the
disaster, escaped from this battle-field, but before
long both he and his colleague in guilt, Maximus,
fell victims to the righteous vengeance of the Goths[1].

That day, that fatal day of the banquet at Marcianople, 'took away,' says the Gothic historian, 'the
hunger of the Goths and the security of the Romans; and the former now began, not as strangers
and foreigners, but as citizens and lords, to issue
their orders to the cultivators of the soil, and to hold
all the northern regions [from the Balkans] to the
Danube in their own right.'

[1] Jordanes xxvi: 'Illico in ducum Lupicini et Maximi armantur
occisionem.'

377–378.
*Gothic
War.*

The war thus commenced lasted, with varying success, through the years 377 and 378. The Emperor Valens, during the whole of the former year, remained at Antioch, but sent two officers of high rank, but of no great military skill, to conduct the campaign in his stead. On the whole, however, the fortune of war must have been unfavourable to the Goths (who evidently fought with more fury than science), since the chief battle of this year was

377.
*Battle of
Ad Salices.*

fought at a place called Ad Salices (the Willows), as far north as the region now known as the Dobrudscha. Our chief historian [1] (himself long an officer of rank in the Imperial army) gives a striking description of the Gothic warriors, encamped in the centre of a rampart of waggons, and revelling in the abundance of the booty which they had carried off from the wasted plains of Thrace. All night the two armies lay encamped near to one another in sleepless suspense. With the dawn of day the barbarians made an attempt to reach some higher ground, from whence they might rush down on the enemy ; but this manœuvre was checked by a well-executed counter-movement of the legions. As both armies halted and gazed at one another with scowling faces, the Romans raised their martial song (itself borrowed from other barbarians), which was known as the *barritus*, and which, beginning in a low bass key, rose, as it were, by steps to a shrill and exultant treble. The barbarians answered by the old war-songs (discordant in Roman ears, but

[1] Ammianus.

in which our Saxon forefathers would probably have 377–378.
found familiar music), wherein they sang the praises
of their glorious ancestors, sprung from the seed of
gods, and dear to Odin.

Then the battle was joined, and the marshy willow-
intersected plain was seen covered with every phase
of human agony; but all was din and confusion,
and if any well-concerted plan was formed or
executed on either side, it does not appear in the
pages of the historian. The battle was a drawn
one; but apparently the Romans were left in
possession of the field, for their dead were buried,
while the bodies of the Goths were left to be de-
voured by vultures. Years after, the husbandman,
ploughing in that fatal plain, marvelled at the mighty
bones of the barbarians which his plough-share up-
turned.

In this battle good service had been rendered by *Advance of*
some troops which Gratian had sent from Gaul to *Gratian.*
the assistance of his uncle. The young Emperor
had had his own hard battles to fight with the barbarians who dwelt on the northern shore of the Lake
of Constance, but having subdued them he marched
eastwards in 378 as far as Sirmium on the Save,
from which place he sent a message to Valens that
he was ready to co-operate with him in an attack on
the Goths, whose invasion seemed to imperil the
very existence of the eastern portion of the Empire.

But Valens, who had by this time quitted Antioch *378.*
for Constantinople, was jealous of his young nephew's *Valens at*
fame, and in no humour to add one needless leaf of *Hadrian-*
ople.

378.

laurel to his crown. He had pitched his camp near Hadrianople, and there received the messengers of Gratian, who earnestly besought him to wait for their master's arrival. So Victor advised, a Slavonic barbarian by birth, but master of the Imperial cavalry, and a careful and cautious general. So, however, did not advise his other chief general Sebastian, who was elated by some recent victories that he had won over the barbarians: and his rash counsels found too sure an echo in the jealous heart of Valens. It was decided to fight at once and end the Gothic war by the unaided forces of the East.

Negotia-
tions be-
tween Fri-
tigern and
Valens.

But Fritigern on his side had allies whose arrival he was expecting. The Ostrogothic chiefs, Alatheus and Saphrax, were on their march to join him, and he would fain postpone the battle till they arrived. He therefore sent a Christian priest on an embassy to Valens, offering to make peace if he and his followers might be allowed to occupy Thrace as subjects of the Empire. Nothing came of these negotiations; nothing was meant to come of them; but time was gained for Alatheus and Saphrax to accomplish another day's march towards the army of Fritigern.

Battle of
Hadrian-
ople, 9 Aug.
378.

On the 9th August, 378, a day long and fatally memorable in the annals of the Empire, the legions of Valens moved forth from their entrenched camp under the walls of Hadrianople, and after a march of eight miles under the hot sun of August came in sight of the barbarian vanguard, behind which

stretched the circling line of the waggons that 378.
guarded the Gothic host.

Yet another embassy did the artful Fritigern
(perhaps not over-confident of victory) send into
the Roman camp. There were discussions as to
the dignity and powers of the messengers: the Goth
was willing to send one of his noblest chiefs if the
Roman would do the same as a pledge of his safety.
Richomer, Count of the Domestics, Gratian's representative, expressed his willingness to go as a
hostage into the barbarian camp, but scarcely had
he reached it when, behold! fresh standards were
seen upon the surrounding hills. The long-waited
for troops of Alatheus and Saphrax had arrived, and
not pausing in their headlong career fell like a
thunderbolt on the Roman flank.

The soldiers of the Empire, hot, thirsty, wearied
out with hours of waiting under the blaze of an
August sun, and only half understanding that the
negotiations were ended and the battle begun, fought
at a terrible disadvantage, but fought not ill. The
infantry on the left wing seem even to have pushed
back their enemies and penetrated to the Gothic
waggons. But they were for some reason not
covered as usual by a force of cavalry, and they
were jammed into a too narrow space of ground
where they could not use their spears with effect,
yet presented a terribly easy mark to the Gothic
arrows. They fell in dense masses as they had
stood. Then the whole weight of the enemy's attack
was directed against the centre and right. When

the evening began to close in, the utterly routed
Roman soldiers were rushing in disorderly flight
from the fatal field. The night, dark and moon-
less, may have protected some, but more met their
death rushing blindly over a rugged and unknown
country.

Fate of
Valens.
Meanwhile, Valens had sought shelter with a little
knot of soldiers (the two regiments of Lancearii and
Mattiarii), who still remained unmoved amidst the
surging sea of ruin. When their ranks too were
broken, and when some of his bravest officers had
fallen around him, he joined the common soldiers
in their headlong flight. Struck by a Gothic arrow
he fell to the ground, but was carried off by some of
the eunuchs and life-guardsmen who still accompanied him, to a peasant's cottage hard by. The
Goths, ignorant of his rank, but eager to strip the
gaily-clothed guardsmen, surrounded the cottage and
attempted in vain to burst in the doors. Then mounting to the roof they tried to smoke out the imprisoned
inmates, but succeeding beyond their desires, set fire
to the cottage, and Emperor, eunuchs, and life-
guards perished in the flames. Only one of
the body-guard escaped, who climbed out through
one of the blazing windows and fell into the
hands of the barbarians. He told them when it
was too late what a prize they had missed in their
cruel eagerness, nothing less than the Emperor of
Rome.

Ecclesiastical historians for generations delighted
to point the moral of the story of Valens, that he who

had seduced the whole Gothic nation into the heresy 378.
of Arius, and thus caused them to suffer the punishment of everlasting fire, was himself by those very
Goths burned alive on the terrible 9th of August.

LECTURE IV.

THEODOSIUS.

378.   In the battle of Hadrianople two-thirds of the Roman army fell. The two Counts, Sebastian and Trajan (the General-in-Chief and his predecessor), Valerian, the Count of the Imperial Stables, and Aequitius, a relation of the Emperor and Superintendent of his palace [1], were all stretched dead upon the field. There too lay thirty-five Tribunes, officers whose military rank corresponded with that of our Colonels. The historian says, with perfect truth, that since the day of Cannae no such disaster had befallen the Roman army. Nor had the Roman State, now in the twelfth century of its existence, the same power of recovering from its reverses which it possessed in the sixth century from the building of the City, when the statue of Victory in the Capitol drooped her wings at the news of the slaughter on the Apulian plain.

Movements of the Goths after the battle of Hadrianople.   Yet the Goths, though they had shown that they could win a battle, had as yet neither discipline nor warlike art sufficient to enable them to conquer in a campaign. An unsuccessful attack on Hadrianople was followed by an equal failure before the walls of

[1] Cura Palati.

Constantinople. By a strange inversion of its future *378.*
fates, the Imperial capital by the Bosphorus was *Siege of*
defended from these Visigoths (the ancestors of *Constan-*
tinople.
Don John of Austria and of all the Christian chivalry
of Spain) by a body of Saracen soldiers who had
been enlisted under the banners of the Empire. One
of these wild defenders of civilisation, nearly naked
but with long and shaggy hair, dashed forward
with a melancholy howl into the Gothic ranks,
stabbed an enemy with his short sword, and then
putting his lips to the neck of the slain foe
sucked his life-blood with eager zest. The thought
of fighting against such monsters as this was too
terrible for the impressionable Goths, and they
retired disheartened from the walls.

But, quite independently of any such exceptional *Weakness*
causes of panic, there was a striking weakness in *of the Goths*
as besiegers.
the Gothic attack whenever they came face to face
with a fenced city. When Fritigern marched away
from the treacherous city of Marcianople, crying
out, 'I wage no war on stone walls,' he expressed
that which was of necessity the maxim of all the barbarian warriors during the succeeding century. It
cannot be said that at this time the powers of the
defence in sieges were necessarily superior to those
of the attack. On the contrary, in the wars between
Persia and Rome it is remarkable how often the
same cities were taken and retaken. But a siege required patience, mechanical skill, and untiring vigilance, and could not be decided by a mere outburst
of Berserker fury such as sometimes swept the

378.

legions before it on the field of battle. In reading the account of a Roman siege-train given by Ammianus Marcellinus[1], though I cannot say that I understand all his explanations (and I believe it would require the combination of an expert mechanician and an invincible translator of Latin to make sense of many of them), still it is easy to perceive this much—that a siege was then, as now, practically a duel of artillery, though in the working of that artillery the explosive force of gunpowder was not made use of, and that it was by the engineer, rather than by the warrior, that the strongest city was

A Roman siege-train. taken. There was the *Balista,* for the discharge of the strong iron-shod wooden arrow; the *Scorpion,* or the *Wild Ass*[2], which suddenly reared itself high in air and hurled forth its heavy stone; the *Battering Ram*[3], for butting at all the weakest places in a wall; the *City-taker*[4], which fastened its triangular prongs into the wall and tore it to pieces. By these and by the great moving towers the city was attacked, and by machines as complicated and as destructive, but of a somewhat different kind, it was defended. For all this sort of work, as I have said, not only the humbler qualities of the soldier— patience and vigilance—but also some of the skill of a trained mechanician, were needed; and these qualities, abundantly present in many even of the common soldiers among the Italians, the Greeks, and the Persians, were yet wanting in the untutored brains of the Teutonic warriors.

[1] xxiii. 4.   [2] Onager.   [3] Aries.   [4] Helepolis.

Therefore the story of the wars between the bar- 378-9.
barians and the Empire is for the most part a story
of monotonous uniformity of ill-success, as far as the
sieges undertaken by the former are concerned. They
win battles in the open field ; they occupy the great
Roman roads, and cut off communication between
the provinces and the capital ; they lay waste the
country districts, and sometimes by the famine thus
caused they deprive the citizens of the means of
prolonging their resistance. More often, by the
treachery of slaves or fellow-countrymen of their
own inside the walls, they bring about the city's
fall ; but scarcely ever do they take it by fair and
open warfare, in a regularly-conducted siege. And
for a considerable part of those seventy years of
struggle which I am briefly describing to you, you
must think of the cities as standing up behind their
quadrangular walls, little islands of civilisation and
still unshaken loyalty to the Empire, while over the
fields and through the unwalled villages rages the
wide-sweeping flood of barbarian invasion.

This was essentially the character of the war *The Gothic*
during the years 378 and 379, though the Roman *attack*
defence was gradually becoming stronger, and the *grows*
attacks of the Goths wilder and more purposeless *feebler,*
during the whole of that period. The despair and *378–339.*
the hatred which had banded them together as one
man under the leadership of Fritigern, lost their
uniting power. They roamed southwards into the
pleasant lands of Achaia, northwards to the Save,
into and perhaps across the borders of Pannonia ;

378-9.   but the hope of plunder and a child's love of breaking beautiful things seem to have been their only
motives.   There is no longer a trace of that serious
purpose of conquest which does seem to have
animated them up to the day of Hadrianople.

The Gothic hostage-boys massacred.   One vile deed of a Roman official must have stirred
many Gothic hearts to fury, yet did not receive its
proper meed of vengeance.   It will be remembered
that when the Visigothic warriors were ferried across
the Danube in the Imperial cutters, they were compelled to deliver up the sons of the noblest among
them as hostages.   These lads had been distributed
through the cities of the East: while their fathers and
their kindred had been suffering the hardships of
famine, they had been growing up to manhood, and
it was feared that the news of the victory of Hadrianople might arouse them to some deed of daring
against the Empire.   Julius, Master of the Soldiery[1],
to whose care these young hostages had been especially committed, sent for the various military prefects, and after binding them to secrecy under solemn
oaths, communicated to them his bloody purpose.
The young Goths in each district were invited to the
capital of the province under promise of receiving
grants of money and land from the Emperor.   They
came full of hope and of good-humour towards their
hosts.   As soon as they were all collected in the
forum of each city, the soldiers, who had been previously stationed on the roofs of the surrounding
houses, assailed them with darts and stones.   They

[1] 'Trans Taurum.' I suppose this is equivalent to 'per Orientem.'

were of course utterly unable to strike a blow in 378-9.
return against their cowardly assailants, and each
Asiatic forum soon had its heap of unresisting slain.
A base and treacherous deed, and one which we
regret to find both our two chief historians[1] of this
period mentioning with words of praise for its
cowardly contrivers.

The disorganisation of the Empire after the battle *Gratian*
of Hadrianople was complete, and Gratian wisely *associates*
Theodosius
concluded that he, a lad of nineteen, was not able, *in the*
unaided, to bring it to a close. He looked around *Imperial*
dignity.
him for a colleague, and recognised with the frank-
ness of his noble nature that there was no man so
suitable for the post as one whom his family had
deeply wronged, the late Duke of Moesia, THEODOSIUS.

This man, whose name in various ways has be- *Origin of*
come so famous in the history both of the Empire *Theodo-*
sius.
and the Church, was born about the year 346 at a
place called Cauca, in the north-western corner of
Spain. He belonged by birth to the class of wealthy
Provincials from which many of the officials of the
Empire were chosen, and who constituted in fact, if
not in name, a sort of rural nobility. After he had
been clothed with the purple, flatterers and poets
discovered that he was a remote descendant of the
great Emperor Trajan, but this seems to have been
only a courtier-like deduction from the fact that he,
like Trajan, was a Spaniard.

[1] Ammianus, ‘Efficacia Julii magistri militiae trans Taurum
enituit salutaris et velox.’ Zosimus, Ἰούλιος τοιῷδέ τινι τρόπῳ τὸν
ἐπηρτημένον ταῖς πόλεσιν ἀποσείεται κίνδυνον.

368-376.   His father, Count Theodosius, had been sent to
Theodosius Britain in 368 to repel an invasion of Picts, Scots,
the Elder.
and Attacotti, and making the old town of Lun-
dinium his base of operations, had attacked the
various parties of freebooters who were roaming
about the country, and had succeeded in spoiling the
spoilers, and restoring the greater part of their property to the plundered provincials.   Two years
afterwards he had delivered Raetia (Tyrol and the
Grisons) from a similar invasion of the Alamanni,
and had sent many of the invaders to Italy to cultivate as serfs the meadow lands of the Po.   In 373
he conducted a most successful campaign in Africa
against a Mauritanian chieftain, Firmus, who had
rebelled against the Emperor.   The rebel committed
suicide, and his conqueror, with the title of *Comes
Africae*, administered the government of the province
which he had saved.   Then came a sudden check to
his prosperous course.   In 376, shortly after the
death of Valentinian, he was accused, we know not
on what charge, sentenced to death, and beheaded
at Carthage, having first received the sacrament of
baptism.   The cause of this strange and sad termination of an honourable career has never been explained.   Some think that the young Gratian, only
just arrived at the helm of affairs, was jealous of the
veteran's fame, but nothing in the character of that
Emperor justifies so foul a charge.   Others believe
that his real offence was having exposed the villainies
and peculations of Romanus, his predecessor in the
government of Africa.   But it seems to me on the

whole most probable that his death was in some 376-379.
way connected with an outburst of jealous rage and
suspicion on the part of Valens against all persons
whose names began with the letters THEOD, Theo-
dorus, Theodoret, and so forth, as it had come to
the ears of the Emperor that a citizen of Antioch
had been resorting to magical arts to learn the name
of his future successor, and that those letters (which
proved fatal to many a Roman citizen) had been
revealed by the oracle as forming the beginning of
the fated name.

On the death of his father, the young Theodosius,
then about thirty years of age, who had done good
service to the State as Duke of Moesia, retired into
private life. If, as was probably the case, he was
succeeded by the base and corrupt Maximus, whose
avarice drove the Goths to despair, the unjust death
of the elder Theodosius was indeed soon and terribly
avenged on his ungrateful masters.

Now, however, the fortunes of the house of Theo- *Theodosius*
dosius emerged from the cloud, more resplendent *Emperor of*
the East,
than ever. The new Emperor was clothed in the *19 Jan.*
purple and invested with 'the rule of the universe' *379.*
(ἡ τῶν ὅλων ἀρχή) at Sirmium, on the 19th of January,
379. The share of the Empire assigned to his immediate superintendence was of course the East,
together with Macedonia and Dacia. The rest of
the Diocese of Illyricum was joined, now as on
many other occasions, to the Western half of the
Empire.

The first duty that Theodosius had to undertake *Guerilla*
War.

379-380. was to restore the self-confidence and trust in victory of the Roman army, terribly shaken as these qualities had been by the disastrous rout of Hadrianople. This he accomplished by waging a successful guerilla war with the Gothic marauders. Valens had played into the hands of the barbarians by risking everything on one great pitched battle. Theodosius adopted the very opposite policy. He outmanœuvred the isolated and straggling bands of the Goths, defeated them in one skirmish after another that did not deserve the name of a battle, and thus restored the courage and confidence of the Imperial troops. By the end of 379 he seems to have succeeded in clearing the territory south of the Balkan range of the harassing swarms of the barbarians.

Sickness of Theodosius.

In February, 380, he fell sick at Thessalonica (which was his chief basis of operations throughout this period), and this sickness, from which he did not fully recover for some months, was productive of two important results, (1) his baptism as a Trinitarian Christian, (2) a renewal of the war against fresh swarms of barbarians.

Theodosius adopts the Creed of Nicaea.

(1) Theodosius appears up to this point of his career not to have definitely ranged himself on either side of the great Arian controversy, though he had a hereditary inclination towards the Creed of Nicaea. Like his father, however, he had postponed baptism in accordance with the prevalent usage of his day: but now upon a bed of sickness which seemed likely to be one of death, he delayed no longer, but received the rite at the hands of

Ascholius, the Catholic Bishop of Thessalonica. 380.
Before he was able to resume his post at the head
of the legions, he published his celebrated Edict:
'To the people of Constantinople.—We desire that
all the nations who are governed by the rule of our
Clemency shall practise that religion which the Apostle
Peter himself delivered to the Romans, and which
it is manifest that the pontiff Damasus, and Peter,
Bishop of Alexandria, a man of Apostolic sanctity,
do now follow: that according to the discipline of
the Apostles and the teaching of the Evangelists
they believe in the one Godhead of Father, Son,
and Holy Spirit, in equal Majesty, and in the holy
Trinity. We order all who follow this law to assume
the name of Catholic Christians, decreeing that all
others, being mad and foolish persons, shall bear the
infamy of their heretical dogmas, and that their Con-
venticles shall not receive the name of Churches: to
be punished first by Divine vengeance, and afterwards by that exertion of our power to chastise
which we have received from the decree of heaven.'

Thus then at length the Caesar of the East was *The power*
ranged on the side of Trinitarian orthodoxy. Con- *of the East-*
stantine in the latter part of his reign, Constantius, *ern State*
Valens, had all been Arians or semi-Arians, some of *now en-*
them bitter in their heterodoxy. Julian had been a *the side of*
worshipper of the gods of Olympus. Thus for nearly *Orthodoxy.*
two generations the influence of the Court of Constantinople had been thrown into the scale against
the teaching of Athanasius, which was generally
accepted throughout the Western realm. Now by

380.

the accession of Theodosius to the Trinitarian side, religious unity was restored to the Empire : but at the same time a chasm, an impassable chasm, was opened between the Empire itself and its new Teutonic guests, nearly all of whom held fast to the Arian teaching of their great Apostle Ulfilas.

Further inroads of the barbarians.

(2) The other consequence of the sickness of Theodosius was, as I have said, a fresh incursion of barbarian hordes, swarming across the Danube and climbing all the high passes of the Balkans. The work of clearing the country of these marauders had to be all done over again. One dark night, when the Emperor was encamping in Macedonia, the barbarians, seeing a particularly bright watch-fire burning, and rightly conjecturing that it marked the tent of the Emperor, made a sudden dash and very nearly succeeded in sending Theodosius to rejoin his predecessor Valens. There was a terrible struggle : few Romans against the overwhelming hosts of the Goths, but the soldiers of Theodosius, who loved him well, fought on desperately till he had escaped, and then fell dead, surrounded by an uncounted host of slain barbarians.

Reinforcements sent by Gratian, 380.

The campaign of 380 was such a hard one that Theodosius had to solicit reinforcements from his colleague Gratian, which were sent to him under the command of Bauto and Arbogast, two Frankish chiefs who had entered the Imperial service. Indeed all along the line, in the West as in the East, the characteristic feature of this period was the number of barbarians who attained high rank in the legions

of Rome, and who upon the whole served her with 380-381.
marked fidelity.

At length, in the closing months of 380, the
provinces south of the Balkans (Macedonia and
Thrace) were once more cleared of their barbarian
intruders. Peace, in which Gratian concurred, was
concluded with the Goths who still doubtless a-
bounded in Moesia; and Theodosius on the 24th
of November entered Constantinople in state.

The inhabitants of the New Rome by the Bosphorus, *Theodosius*
who perhaps had not before seen Theodosius as *welcomes*
Emperor, were soon to behold a ruler of a very *Athanaric*
different type side by side with the courtly and *at Constan-*
magnificent Spaniard. The grey old Visigoth, Atha- *tinople,*
naric, had been driven, apparently by Ostrogothic *381.*
invaders, from his airy stronghold in the Carpathians. The death of Fritigern (which seems
to have happened about this time) left him the chief
ruler of the scattered and disorganised Visigothic
nation. Converted from his old, almost religious
prejudice against Rome, and recanting the oath
which he had once sworn never to set foot on the
soil of the Empire, he now crossed the Danube and
accepted the Emperor's invitation to visit him in
his capital, probably in order to ratify and proclaim
to the world the peace just concluded between
'Romania' and 'Gothia.' We must let the Gothic
historian tell the story of this visit in his own ex-
pressive words [1].

'Theodosius attached to himself King Athanaric,

[1] Jordanes xxviii.

381.

who had succeeded Fritigern, by the gifts which he gave him, and in the kindest terms invited him to visit him at Constantinople ; who accepted right willingly and said, marvelling, "Lo, I behold, what often I heard incredulously, the fame of so great a city." Then turning his eyes this way and that, now he admires the position of the city and the concourse of ships, now the long clearly-marked line of the walls, and then again the natives from so many different stocks bubbling up like water from one fountain in many directions, yet all disciplined like well-trained soldiers. "A god," he said, "without doubt a god upon earth is the Emperor, and whoever moveth a hand against him, that man is guilty of his own blood." In such a state of admiration, being supported by the yet greater honours which he received from the Emperor, after the interval of a few months [or more correctly fourteen days[1]] he departed from the light of day.

Athanaric's death. Whom the Emperor out of the love which he bore to him, honouring almost more as dead than as alive, delivered to a worthy burial, himself going before the bier in his solemn obsequies. Therefore when Athanaric was dead, all his army, remaining in the service of the Emperor Theodosius, and submitting itself to the Roman Empire, formed as it were one body with the [Imperial] soldiery, that old enlistment of the Foederati under the Emperor Constantine being now renewed, and they themselves were now called Foederati.'

[1] Idatius, Descriptio Consulum, makes the entry of Athanaric into Constantinople 11 Jan. and his death 25 Jan. 381.

There can be no doubt that the politic courtesy *The bulk* which Theodosius showed to Athanaric exercised an *of the Goths* important influence on the relations which existed *Foederati* for the next fifteen years between the Empire and *of the Em-* the Goths. If we look at the position of the two *pire.* parties to the contract we shall see that the conclusion or the renewal of the *Foedus* between them was really for the interest of both. For the Empire, a complete reversal of the policy of Valens was now impossible. Ever since the day when the last of the 200,000 Gothic warriors was ferried across the Danube, their inclusion in the Empire in one capacity or another had become an accomplished and irreversible fact. They could not be thrust back into their old Dacian home, where by this time the Huns were probably swarming, but they might be converted from the ravagers of Thrace into the tillers of Moesia. They might be made the stalwart defenders of the Danubian frontier against those very Huns, and against the motley horde of Teutons, Slaves, and Tartars who flocked around their standard of squalid and anarchic despotism.

On the other hand the Goths, unable to capture the strong cities of the Empire, could not live perpetually on the mere ravage of the Thracian home-steads. Viewing the movements of peoples and the migrations of barbarous tribes from the high historic standpoint, and especially seeing what these movements and migrations actually accomplished in the fifth century of our era, we are apt to think that the conquest of kingdoms and the foundation of empires was the deliberate and persistent purpose of chief and people. On the contrary, if we could be present in the rough councils which gathered around their camp-fires and listen to the talk of the warriors with their wives in the great Gothic waggons, we should probably discover that the question in what way and from what source the next day's meal was to be provided, was far more often and more anxiously debated than any question of high policy or dream of world-conquest. Now, by the policy which Theodosius seemed willing to adopt of renewing the old *Foedus* between Rome and her Gothic friends, food, and comfortable homes, and a distinguished career in arms were assured to the meanest Gothic soldier, and admission to the dignities and luxuries of the most splendid court in the world was assured to their chiefs. The Roman Empire was still, if I may use a commercial phrase, ' a going concern.' The barbarians had power to wreck it and drive it into bankruptcy? Yes, perhaps they had: but it was surely a far more alluring prospect to take shares in the company and touch some part of the enormous profits which accrued to the directors.

This kind of calculation—and I have purposely chosen a commercial metaphor in order to indicate the perfectly selfish character of the bargain— prevailed at this time in the minds of the barbarians over any dim and shadowy dreams which might linger there of setting up a new and conquering Visigothic kingdom between the Danube and the

Balkans. But then, when self-interest was prompting
them to this course, sentiment was enlisted on the
same side by the generous hospitality offered to the
worn-out veteran Athanaric in the great city of the
South, by his own childlike admiration of the wonders
which she displayed to his view, by the splendid
funeral, and by the sight of the courtly Augustus,
robed in the purple and wearing the diadem of Empire, escorting the Gothic warrior to his tomb.

What the precise nature of the tie was which *What did*
bound the *foederati* to the Empire I do not think *the relation*
we can definitely explain. From time immemorial *rati in-*
of Foede-
Rome had fought her battles with troops pretty *volve?*
equally divided between the legions (theoretically
composed of pure Roman citizens) and the *Auxilia*
(consisting of her subject-allies). These allies had
at first been chiefly dwellers in the cities of Latium,
but by the time that we have now reached they were
gathered from almost every nation under heaven.
Here, in our own Northumberland, all the garrison
duty along the Wall was done by these auxiliary
troops. Asturians from Spain, Tungrians and Bata-
vians from Holland, Dacians from Transylvania, and
Dalmatians from the eastern shore of the Hadriatic,
were keeping watch for Rome on these wind-swept
hills. But *those* allies were still distinctly Roman
soldiers, who served under Roman officers, and
were amenable to Roman discipline. The bond
which held the *foederati* to the Empire appears to
have been a much looser one. It would seem that
the federated Goths still served under their own

native chiefs, and retained to a large extent their
national weapons and their own peculiar manner of
fighting. They no doubt had lands assigned to
them, chiefly in Moesia, which they may have culti-
vated partly with their own hands and partly by the
forced labour of *coloni.* In fact, though we are of
course still many centuries off from regular feudal
rights and obligations, there was probably something
in the relation of a chief of *foederati* to the Emperor
not altogether unlike the relation of a feudal baron
to his lord paramount.

*Results of
the policy
of Theodo-
sius.*

The scheme of Theodosius answered as a temporary expedient. It gave security to the Danubian
frontier for his day; perhaps had his successors
been men of equal ability with himself it might have
prolonged that security for centuries. But there
were some obvious dangers attending it. Evidently
these masses of men, trained to act together, obeying
their own princes, and conscious of their strength,
might one day turn against Rome the weapons which
they were now wielding on her behalf. The 'provincials,' the earlier subjects of Rome, finding their
services less needed, would grow unused to warfare,
and would in the course of time be almost sure to
sink into a despised and spiritless caste, among
whom the proud Teutonic *foederatus* would stalk
with an exasperating consciousness of superiority.
Above all, the Emperor himself, having the barbarians for his tent companions, the sharers of his
dangers, the confidants of his councils, and the sup-
porters of his throne, would get to lean more and

more upon them, and might become an Emperor of
barbarians instead of an Emperor of the civilised
commonwealth of Rome.

The whole history of Theodosius shows that
this was a very real danger in his time. There
was something in his own character, fond as he
was of pomp and spectacle and the mere outward
trappings of royalty, which harmonised only too well
with the nature of the barbarians. While he was
surrounding himself with troops of tall and bril-
liantly-accoutred *foederati,* and spending his time and
the money of his subjects over an endless round of
games and chariot-races, and on sumptuous ban-
quets at which the Gothic 'wassail' was loudly
heard, the provinces were groaning under the
demands of the tax-gatherer; and the machine
of administration which Valens, with all his faults,
had superintended with some diligence, was daily
getting into more and more hopeless disorganisation.

Both the two great insurrections which broke out *Insurrec-*
in the reign of Theodosius, and each of which is *tion of*
Antioch,
connected with the story of a great father of the 387.
Church, sprang, directly or indirectly, from the
favour shown by the Emperor to his *foederati.* In
the year 387 he determined to celebrate the fifth
year of the reign of his young son Arcadius, whom
he had associated with him in the Empire, in a style
of extraordinary magnificence. For this purpose
there must be more splendid games, more exciting
chariot-races, and, above all, a more liberal donative

387.   to the soldiery than any that had yet been given.
In order to supply funds for these various ex-
penses, a new tax (probably what was called the
aurum coronarium) was levied on the cities of the
Empire.   At the news of this fresh imposition, the
citizens of Antioch, already ground down to the very
dust by the pressure of the ordinary taxation, broke
out into open rebellion.   While the more respect-
able and religious citizens betook themselves to the
churches to pray God to change the Emperor's
purpose, or besought the Bishop Flavianus to intercede for the removal of the tax, a mob of boys and
'lewd fellows of the baser sort' visited the spacious
Baths, and cutting the ropes by which the lamps were
suspended, caused them to fall with a crash on the
pavement.   Then the boys began to throw stones at
the wooden statues of the Emperor and his family.
They shouted for joy when one of the statues was
split in pieces ; they groaned when one, more stubborn than the rest, long resisted their assaults.
They then went to the more costly bronze statues,
pulled them from their pedestals with ropes, dragged
them ignominiously through the streets, and ended
by giving them to the children to play with.   What
made the insult the more bitter was, that not only
the statues of the Emperor himself, but those of the
noble old veteran his father, of his lately deceased
wife, and of his young son and colleague, were all
treated with the same contumely.   Next came an
attempt at fire-raising in the house of a magistrate
who tried to persuade them to cease their rioting ;

and last, the appearance of some Imperial archers, 387.
who discharged their arrows upon the crowd. Thereupon at once the tumult, which had flamed up so
high and seemed so menacing, died down like a fire
of straw.

The insult to the majesty of the Emperor had been *Reaction*
great, perhaps unforgiveable. The whole city passed *from in-*
solence to
in an hour from the extreme of insolence and an- *panic.*
archy to the extreme of cowed submission and abject
terror, while the messengers bearing the fatal tidings
were going to and returning from Constantinople.
The sedition had broken out a few days before Lent
(387), and the whole of the forty days of that sacred
season were indeed days of fasting and humiliation
to the luxurious citizens of Antioch. About the
middle of them arrived a letter from the Emperor,
sharply rebuking the Town Council for allowing
the sedition to gain such a height, ordering that the
Theatre, the Hippodrome, and the Baths should all
be closed, and depriving Antioch of the rank, which
she had held for six centuries, as capital of Syria.
Shortly after appeared two Imperial Commissioners
—Caesarius and Ellebichus—charged to make enquiry into the recent events; and they began their
enquiry by putting all the Senators of Antioch into
close confinement.

The two commissioners, however, were specimens *Pardon.*
of the best class of Roman officials, men utterly unlike Lupicinus and Maximus. They marked the
sincere repentance and the agonised prostration of
terror which pervaded all classes in Antioch, and

they soon allowed it to appear that their influence at any rate would be exerted on the side of mercy. Caesarius, when the enquiry was completed, set off with all speed to Constantinople, and reached that city on the sixth day after his departure from Antioch. No Turkish courier probably could now traverse the length and breadth of Asia Minor in anything like so short a time. Theodosius listened to the arguments of Caesarius in favour of mercy, to the prayers and sighs of Bishop Flavianus, who had come to intercede on behalf of his flock, and granted a complete amnesty, rescinding also his previous decree for the degradation of Antioch from the rank of capital city. This letter, carried by a swift messenger to Ellebichus, was by him communicated to the citizens of Antioch, who received it with shouts of welcome and tears of joy. Their fifty days of mourning were ended, and Antioch, the light-hearted Paris of the East, was herself again.

The story of this singular insurrection has been preserved for us by the orations of the heathen sophist Libanius and by the homilies of the great Christian preacher, St. John Chrysostom, at that time a priest at Antioch, afterwards Patriarch of Constantinople.

*Insurrec-
tion of
Thessa-
lonica,
390.*

The insurrection at Antioch displayed the character of Theodosius in a favourable light, as a strong but merciful and magnanimous ruler of men. Very different was the effect on his fame of the insurrection which broke out three years later (390) in the Macedonian city of Thessalonica. A garrison of Gothic

foederati was quartered in this important city. Al- 390.
ready it is probable that many causes of quarrel
had arisen between the Thessalonians and their
overbearing but under-educated guests. The wrath
grew to its height when Botheric, the Gothic general,
shut up in prison a certain scoundrel of a charioteer
who had vilely insulted him. At the next races the
mob of Thessalonica tumultuously demanded the
charioteer's liberation, and when Botheric refused,
rose in insurrection and slew both him and several
magistrates of the city. There was no such direct
insult to the person of the Emperor as at Antioch,
perhaps no such prolonged period of defiance to
authority; but the affair reflected deep disgrace on
the cruel, childish, show-loving Eastern provincials,
and if the chief actors in it had been ordered off to
instant execution, Theodosius would only have acted
with praiseworthy severity. But he had now been *Brutal*
for twelve years lord of the world, and the madness *vengeance.*
which absolute power so often brings with it had
begun to work in his brain. In a frenzy of rage at
the insult offered to himself in the person of his
barbarian general, he sent his orders from Milan
(where he was staying when the tidings reached him)
that the whole city of Thessalonica should suffer for
the misdeeds of its ruffianly mob. The soldiers
surrounded the circus where the citizens were assembled, watching the games and unsuspecting of
ill. They closed the gates, marched in amongst the
densely-packed spectators, and began their bloody
work. A certain number of heads was ordered to

390.

be brought to the officers, as if they had been thistles or dandelions to be gathered out of the fields. Was it 7000 as one historian says, or 15,000, as another? It matters not much: the horror of the thing was the brutal indiscriminateness of the massacre, the utter absence of any attempt to separate between the innocent and the guilty, the indifference to human life, more worthy of Tamerlane and his pyramid of skulls than of an Emperor of Rome.

Penitence of Theodosius.

It is true that this bloody deed was afterwards repented of in dust and ashes. The humiliation and penitence of Theodosius, his self-abasement before the great Christian hero, St. Ambrose, and the forgiveness which he at last received from him, form a well-known page in church history, and one which I do not propose now to retrace. But I cannot hold, as some of the ecclesiastical historians seem to do, that the depth of the Emperor's subsequent humility hides the greatness of his crime. That he should have been even tempted to such a monstrous abuse of his absolute power, much more that he should have yielded to the temptation, marks him out as one of the Emperors who were unfit to govern, not only as immeasurably below a saint like Marcus Aurelius, or a statesman like Trajan, but almost as fit to be classed in the same category with Caligula, Nero, and Commodus.

We return to our more special subject, the relation between Theodosius and the *foederati*. Twice he was able to employ his Gothic soldiers with

striking success in the internal struggles of the 383.
Empire. The situation was thus very similar to
that which we have seen in our own day in our
Indian Empire, when the Sikhs, the fierce opponents
of the English Raj in 1845, became its stalwart
defenders in the terrible Mutiny of 1857.

In the year 383 a military revolt broke out in *Revolt of*
Britain against the young Emperor Gratian. Our *troops in*
island was ever the fruitful seed-plot of these mili- *Britain,*
tary mutinies. The soldiers, shut up in their camps 383.
on our solitary moors, and deeming themselves cut
off from the civilised world [1], probably exaggerated
every hardship of their service, and welcomed any
change which would take them southwards, were it
even in the track of an usurper and a tyrant. Perhaps, too, there was something then as now in the
disposition of the Celts by whom they were surrounded, and with whom many of them had inter-
married, favourable to anarchy and fatal to that
reverence for law and discipline which is needed to
hold together either an army or a state. Whatever the cause, the army revolted and proclaimed
Magnus Clemens Maximus, Emperor. He was, like *Elevation*
Theodosius, a native of Spain, and though harsh and *of Maxi-*
perhaps rapacious, a man of ability and experience, *mus.*
not unworthy of the purple if he had come to it by
lawful means [2]. Gratian on his side had evidently
given some real cause for dissatisfaction to his sub-

---

[1] ' Penitus toto divisos orbe Britannos.'

[2] ' Vir strenuus et probus atque Augusto dignus, nisi contra sacra-
menti fidem per tyrannidem emersisset.'   (Historia Miscella xi. 16.)

383.
*Gratian's
faults.*
jects. Ammianus, who was a good judge of character, says of him that 'while the youthful down was
yet on his cheeks he showed promise of emulating
the best of the Emperors, if he had not given his
mind too much to sport, and under the influence of
frivolous companions followed too much the example
of Commodus in his dissipation though not in his
cruelty. He delighted to pierce the greatest possible number of beasts before the eyes of the people,
and when he had given a fatal wound to each one
of a hundred lions let loose from many doors all
round the amphitheatre (not needing to hit any
beast twice), he would exult as if he were something
more than man. Thus he would spend whole days
within these vast preserves which were called *vi-
varia*, slaying savage beasts with his multitudinous
arrows. And this at a time when even the patient
earnestness of a Marcus Aurelius would have been
all too little for the sad necessities of the Empire[1].'

But there was another grievance besides Gratian's
love for sport, and that was his fondness for the
barbarians. He, too, like Theodosius, had his petted
barbarian guard, but instead of being Goths they
belonged to the less civilised race of the Alani. We
are told by another author[2] 'that Gratian neglected
the army and preferred a few of the Alans, whom by
lavish pay he had attracted to his service, to the old
Roman soldiery, and was so fascinated by the com-
panionship, and one might almost say friendship of
these barbarians, that he sometimes on the march

---

[1] xxxi. 10, 18 and 19.   [2] Historia Miscella xii. 16.

even adopted their dress.   By all this he aroused *383-7.*
the hatred of the soldiers against himself.'

An Emperor of barbarians, an Emperor who was
spending his days in shooting wild beasts while the
Empire was languishing under taxes within and the
attacks of savages from without,—that was the aspect
which, with many noble and loveable qualities,
Gratian bore to his Western subjects : and hence it
was that when Maximus with the army of Britain
landed in Gaul, he shook down the fabric of his
power without difficulty.   Gratian, finding himself *Death of*
deserted by his troops, escaped from the battle-field, *Gratian.*
but was overtaken and killed at Lyons.

For more than four years Maximus, satisfied with *Maximus*
ruling over the three great Western provinces which *dethrones*
Valenti-
had fallen to the share of Gratian, maintained at *nian II,*
any rate the appearance of harmony with his two *387.*
colleagues, and the CONCORDIA AUGGG was still capable of being commemorated on the Imperial medals.
At length, in the autumn of 387, Maximus deemed
that the time had come for grasping the whole
Empire of the West.   Lulling to sleep the suspicions of Valentinian and his mother by embassies
and protestations of friendship, he crossed the Alps
with an army and marched towards Aquileia, where
the young Emperor was then dwelling in order to
be as near as possible to the dominions of his
friendly colleague and protector.   Valentinian did
not await the approach of his rival, but going down
to the port of Grado, took ship and sailed for Thessalonica, his mother and sisters accompanying him.

387.
Valentini-
an's appeal
for help to
Theodo-
sius.

The Emperor and the Senate of Constantinople met the Imperial fugitives at Thessalonica, and discussed the present position of affairs. The Senate seconded the entreaties of Valentinian and his mother, and cried out for vengeance on the murderer of one Emperor and the despoiler of another. Theodosius, who was sincerely averse to war, as his detractors said through indolence, but more probably through that knowledge of the risks and miseries of war which even the most successful general cannot fail to acquire, spoke in favour of peace, and then of course all warlike views were hushed.

Upon this Justina, who was the widow of two Emperors[1], and in whose countenance still lingered the traces of the extraordinary beauty which had fascinated Valentinian I, fell on her knees before Theodosius and besought him not to allow the murder of Gratian to remain unavenged, nor the family of his former benefactor to be utterly ruined. And then she pointed to her daughter Galla,

' Matre pulchra filia pulchrior,'

who was bathed in tears, lamenting the misfortunes of her house. What the entreaties of the mother might have failed to effect, the tears of the daughter accomplished. Theodosius, whose wife Flaccilla had died two years before (385), took Galla for his second wife, and vowed to avenge her wrongs and replace her brother on the throne.

Civil War
between

He was some time in preparing for the campaign,

[1] Magnentius and Valentinian I.

but, when it was opened, he conducted it with vigour and decision. His troops pressed up the Save valley, defeated those of Maximus in two engagements, entered Aemona (Laybach) in triumph, and soon stood before the walls of Aquileia, behind which Maximus was sheltering himself. The city was a strong and almost impregnable one, but a mutiny among the troops of Maximus did away with the necessity for a siege. The soldiers of Theodosius poured into the city, whose gates had been opened to them by the mutineers, and dragged off the usurper, barefooted, with tied hands, in slave's attire, to the tribunal of Theodosius and his young brother-in-law at the third milestone from the city. After Theodosius had in a short harangue reproached him with the evil deeds which he had wrought against the Roman commonwealth, he handed him over to the executioner, by whom he was at once put to death.

388.

Theodosius and Maximus, 388.

Defeat and death of Maximus.

28 July, 388.

There can be little doubt that the rapid and successful movements of Theodosius in this campaign were due in part to the well-trained valour of his *foederati.* We have, however, a more distinct allusion to their services in the next civil war, which was fought six years afterwards on almost the same battle-ground.

On the overthrow of Maximus, Theodosius had with generous magnanimity handed over to Valentinian II the whole of the Western Empire, both his own especial share and that which had formerly been held by his brother Gratian. The young

Valentinian II restored in the West.

388.

Emperor was now seventeen years of age : his mother, Justina, had died apparently on the eve of Theodosius's victory, and he governed, or tried to govern, alone. He seems to have taken up his residence at Trier, the defence of the Gaulish provinces being doubtless recognised as at this time the chief duty of an Emperor of the West. But the actual functions of supreme ruler were discharged, not by this young and somewhat pliable Emperor, *His fac- totum Ar- bogast.* but by a Frankish veteran who stood beside his throne, moving legions and appointing and dis- placing generals at his will. I mentioned that during the sickness of Theodosius the war in Thrace was successfully conducted by two Frankish lieutenants of Gratian, by name Bauto and Arbogast. Bauto died about the year 385, and from that time onwards supreme power in the dominions of Valentinian had been more and more accumulating itself in the hands of the other great Frankish general, Arbogast, a man adored by his soldiers for his valour and experience in war, and for his noble disdain of riches. This man was apparently true to the Empire, true at first in his own rough way to the house of Valentinian. He had followed the young Emperor to exile, and after the victory at Aemona it was his hand that deprived the young Victor, son of the usurper, of life. But knowing his infinite superiority in all the arts of war and government to the young Adonis who was nominally his master, he took no pains to conceal that superiority, and sometimes in the council

chamber itself openly opposed and scoffed at the *392.*
proposals of the Emperor.   In short, this Frankish
warrior was already anticipating by three centuries
the attitude of the Frankish Mayors of the Palace
towards the Merovingian monarchs.   At length Valentinian, unable to bear the barbarian's insolence *Quarrels*
any longer, one day when he was sitting on his *between*
Valenti-
imperial throne, summoning up as much sternness *nian and*
as he could into his boyish countenance, presented *Arbogast.*
Arbogast with a written dismissal from his command
as *Magister Equitum.*   With calm contempt Arbogast
tore the paper in pieces.   'You never gave me this
command,' said he, 'nor will you be able to take it
from me.'   Valentinian drew a sword against the
general as he turned to depart, but the attendant to
whom it belonged checked him from using it.   Hearing the struggle Arbogast returned and asked what
the Emperor had been trying to do.   'To slay my-
self,' moaned the miserable Valentinian, 'because
although Emperor I have no power[1].'

From this day there was open emmity between *Death of*
Valentinian and his Master of the Horse : and not *Valenti-*
nian II,
long after, when the young Emperor was bathing in *15 May,*
the Rhone, near Vienne, some of the servants of *392.*
Arbogast, in the absence of his body-guard who had
gone away to dinner, rushed upon him and strangled
him.   They then tied a handkerchief round his
neck and hung him to a tree, that it might appear
that he had committed sucide.   It was generally

---

[1] Combined from Zosimus and Philostorgius.   Possibly the two
stories relate to different altercations.

392-394. understood, however, that the death of Valentinian
was in truth the deed of Arbogast.

Eugenius The Frankish general, who durst not shock the
Emperor, prejudices of the Roman world by himself assuming
392-394. the purple, hung that dishonoured robe upon the
shoulders of a rhetorician, a confidant, and almost
a dependent of his own, named Eugenius. This
man, like most of the scholars and rhetoricians of
the day, had not abjured the old faith of Hellas.
As Arbogast also was a heathen, though worshipping
Teutonic rather than Olympian gods, this last
revolution looked like a recurrence to the days of
Julian, and threatened the hardly-won supremacy
of Christianity. Thus not only the sad voice of his
wife Galla pleading for vengeance on her brother's
murderers, but, even more, the pious exhortations of
all Christian bishops called on Theodosius to rescue
the Western Empire from the hands of the sophist
and the barbarian. Yet his preparations had to be
long and careful, for he was aware that in Arbogast
he would meet a general who knew as much of the
art of war as himself, perhaps we might say that he
Death of should meet the greatest captain of the age. He left
Galla, 394. not Thrace till June, 394, nearly two years after the
death of Valentinian, and meanwhile, on the very
eve of his departure his young wife Galla died,
leaving a little daughter, whose name afterwards was
famous in the story of the Empire, Galla Placidia.

Theodosius Giving but one day to sorrow and the next
marches to vengeance, Theodosius marched north-west-
against
Eugenius. wards, as before, up the valley of the Save, and

to the city of Aemona. Not there did he meet his 394.
foes, but at a place about thirty miles off, half-way
between Aemona and Aquileia, where the Julian
Alps are crossed, and where a little stream called
the Frigidus (now the Wipbach) burst suddenly
from a limestone hill. Here, then, the battle was
joined between Eugenius with his Frankish patron
and Theodosius with his 20,000 Gothic *foederati*[1]
and the rest of the army of the East. Gainas, Saul,
Bacurius, Alaric were the chief leaders of the Teutonic troops.

The first day of battle fell heavily on the *foederati* *Battle of*
of Theodosius, half of whom were left dead upon the *the Fri-*
gidus,
field. It seemed as if the West were going once more *5 and 6*
to triumph over the East, as if heathenism might even *Sept.* 394.
once more gain the ascendant over Christianity.
That night, however, in prayer Theodosius had a
vision of the Apostles John and Philip, who cheered
him on with the assurance of victory. Next day
Theodosius succeeded in detaching part of the army
of his rival from their allegiance ; and even the elements seemed eager to aid his victory. The impetuous *Bora*, a wind well known in that region,
sprang up from the hills in the rear of his army and
carried their arrows and their javelins with resistless
force into the ranks of the enemy, whose own missiles
recoiled helplessly on themselves. The battle was
won after a terrible struggle. Eugenius was taken
prisoner and carried bound into the presence of
Theodosius, who upbraided him with his heathenism

[1] Jordanes xxviii.

and his share in the murder of Valentinian.
While he was grovelling at the proud conqueror's
feet and begging for mercy, a soldier cut off his head
and carried it round the field of battle on a pole to
show the vanquished army that their Emperor was
slain.   Arbogast wandered about for some days
among the rugged mountain-defiles, and then fell
upon his sword and perished.

Theodosius, who was still in the prime of life, had
now indeed 'the rule of the world,' without a rival or
a colleague except his own boyish sons. The Church
and the federated Goths, two of the most powerful
forces in the Empire, were both devotedly attached
to him ; and the Provincials, though groaning under
the weight of the taxes which he imposed, feared, and
perhaps admired him.   Had his life been prolonged
as it well might have been for twenty or thirty years
longer, many things might have gone differently
in the history of the world.   But, little more than
four months after the victory of the Frigidus, Theo-

dosius died of dropsy at Milan, his constitution being
prematurely worn out by the hardships of his last
campaign, and possibly by the high feasting and
revelry which had resounded through his palace at
Constantinople.   He had probably not yet completed
his fiftieth year.

The character of Theodosius is one of the most
perplexing in history. The Church historians have
hardly a word of blame for him except in the matter
of the massacre of Thessalonica, and that, as has
been said, seems to be almost atoned for in their

eyes by its perpetrator's penitent submission to ecclesiastical censure. On the other hand, the heathen historians, represented by Zosimus, condemn in the most unmeasured terms his indolence, his love of pleasure, his pride, and hint at the scandalous immorality of his life. Varying a similar saying with reference to Constantine, we might say that he who believes all the evil that is said of Theodosius by Socrates, and all the good that is said of him by Zosimus, will not go far wrong. But this takes us only a little way, for the blame and the praise are both infinitesimal.

He had one great work to do, the reconciliation of the Goths to the Empire, and he did that work well. It is perhaps unfair to judge of it by the slenderness of its permanent results, since his early death may have been the chief cause of its failure. But he was certainly passionate, egotistic, cruel. He spared not the pockets of his subjects, and his reign, like a heavy wheat-crop, exhausted the energies of his Empire. It is the fashion to call him the Great, and we may admit that he has as good a right to that title as Louis XIV, a monarch whom in some respects he pretty closely resembles. But it seems to me that it would be safer to withhold this title from both sovereigns, and to call them, not the Great, but the *Magnificent.*

LECTURE V.

Alaric.

Arcadius and Honorius, sons of Theodosius.

Their incapacity.

On the death of Theodosius (395) his two sons, Arcadius and Honorius, aged respectively eighteen and ten, succeeded to 'the rule of the world,' Arcadius dwelling at Constantinople and ruling the Eastern portion, while the Western fell to the share of Honorius, who at this time generally dwelt at Milan. Arcadius died in the year 408, at the age of thirty-one; Honorius in 423, at the age of thirty-nine. These two men were thus nominally at the head of human affairs during some of the most profoundly interesting and important events that have happened in the history of the world; yet few men have ever by their own force of character or strength of intellect exercised less influence on the destinies of the human race. Theodosius, with all his faults, interests the student of his reign: he was brilliant, forceful, and he makes a mark on the history of his time. The dulness of his sons' characters is so portentous, that after the lapse of a millennium and a half the Muse of History still yawns at the remembrance of them. Arcadius had a beautiful Frankish wife, and left a son of artistic temperament,

and four pious daughters. Honorius married his
deceased wife's sister and left no family, but was
fond of keeping pigeons. These are pretty nearly
all the facts that it is possible to ascertain or to
remember out of the drizzling dulness of their
personal history.

Theodosius, who probably saw the weakness of *Adminis-*
character of his sons, and who was leaving them at *tration of*
Rufinus
an age when even strong and capable natures would *and Sti-*
have required much help and guidance, entrusted *licho.*
the guardianship of the lads, and the virtual regency
of the Empire, to Rufinus and Stilicho. The former,
with the rank of Praetorian Prefect, administered
the realm of Arcadius; the latter, as *Magister Utri-*
usque Militiae, governed the army and the people of
Honorius.

These two men resembled one another in one
quality—an inordinate love of money, whether justly
or unjustly acquired. In all other respects their
characters were utterly dissimilar. Stilicho, though
grasping and perhaps somewhat coarse-fibred, was a
hero and a patriot; Rufinus (whom we unfortunately
know only by the descriptions of his bitter enemies)
may have had some administrative ability, but must
have been a bad specimen even of the corrupt
bureaucracy of Constantinople.

Dissimilar as was the character of the two men,
so also was their origin and training. Stilicho was
apparently of pure Teutonic extraction, the son of a
Vandal chief who had commanded some barbarian
auxiliaries in the army of the Emperor Valens.

His tall and handsome presence had commended him to the favour of Serena, the favourite niece and trusted counsellor of Theodosius. His marriage with so near a relative of the Emperor naturally led to his speedy promotion. His employment on an embassy to the Persian king was followed by high military command. He showed indisputable talents for war in several campaigns against the barbarians, and, some years before the death of Theodosius, was raised to the highest of all military dignities—that of *Magister Utriusque Militiae* (Commander-in-Chief of Infantry and Cavalry).

Of the early life of Rufinus we know but little. He was born at Elusa, a little town in the south-west corner of Gaul. He went to Constantinople, and there, by his obsequiousness, his perseverance, and doubtless also by his aptitude for the work of administration, succeeded in climbing from step to step of the official ladder. One or two old and faithful servants of the Empire (Tatianus and Proculus) who stood above him in rank, were cast down by his well-timed accusations of disloyalty, and at length the obscure Gaulish Provincial blazed forth to the world as Praetorian Prefect of the East—one of the wealthiest men in the Empire, a man who aspired to wear the diadem himself as colleague of Arcadius, and to obtain the Emperor's hand in marriage for his daughter. Thus while Stilicho's might be said to be the typical career of a robust, handsome, and warlike Teuton in the service of the Empire, the career of Rufinus was the equally typical career of a clever, pushing, and unscrupulous Provincial.

Between the two administrators of the realm— *Divergence* Rufinus and Stilicho—there was no cordiality, no *between East and* chance of well-concerted action for the good of the *West.* Empire. In fact, quite independently of the personal characters of the two men, the interests of the two divisions of the Empire were now beginning manifestly to diverge. The older Rome looked down upon the new Rome by the Bosphorus as a mere Greek city, the home of sophists and chatterers; while Constantinople regarded the city of the Tiber, with its mouldering palaces, its desolate Campagna, its still half-heathen Senate, as a great stranded hulk, unfit any longer to bear the precious freight of Empire. This divergence between the hopes and wishes of the East and West, a divergence which was often on the point of becoming actual hostility, was wider for the first fifteen years after the death of Theodosius than for a considerable time before or after that interval, and promoted not a little the success of the barbarian movement against the Roman State.

That movement began very shortly after Theo- *Alaric* dosius was laid in his grave. It was in all proba- *King of the Visigoths.* bility in the spring of the year 395 that the Visigoths in Moesia raised the young Alaric upon a shield, and with joyful shouts acclaimed him as their king. We have already noticed this young Gothic chief as commanding a troop in the army of Theodosius at the battle of the Frigidus, and that is in fact

all that we know about him up to this date, except
that he was born (probably between 360 and 370) in
the island of Peuce at the mouth of the Danube, and
that he was either himself surnamed Baltha (the
Bold), or belonged to a clan of kings or chieftains
who bore that name. As the Gothic historian says :
'As soon as Alaric was created king, deliberating
with his people he persuaded them rather by their
own labour to seek for kingdoms than quietly to lie
down in subjection to strangers.' In other words he
decided, and persuaded them to decide, to abandon
the easy but inglorious position of *foederati*, and
cutting themselves loose from the old and decaying
Empire, to hew out new realms for themselves with
their own trusty broadswords. Towards this decision he was no doubt partly guided by what he had
himself seen, when in the Imperial service, of the
weakness of the legions, the unwarlike character of
the Provincials of the Empire, the oppressions of
the tax-gatherers which caused even the barbarians
to seem welcome as deliverers from their yoke ;
above all by what he, and every officer of rank in
the Roman army, knew of the discord and jealousy
between the two chief ministers of the Empire.

The first blows of Alaric and his Goths were
struck at the Eastern Empire. This was natural
enough, since they were themselves settled within
it : but there was another reason for the choice.
The army which Theodosius had led with him across
the Julian Alps seems not to have been dismissed to
its Eastern cantonments during the few months

between the battle of the Frigidus and his death. 395.
It and the troops of Eugenius were now all collected in the north of Italy under the orders of
Stilicho, who was thus in another than the official
sense *Magister Utriusque Militiae*, since both the
conquering and the conquered army of the late
campaign received the watchword from him. A
singular position certainly, and one which excuses
some things otherwise difficult to justify in the conduct of Arcadius and his minister.

Alaric, then, with his Gothic followers marched *Alaric*
first towards Constantinople. Perhaps he had some *strikes at*
the Eastern
hopes of taking the city by surprise, but if so he was *Empire.*
disappointed. Rufinus, who, Provincial as he was,
professed a certain fondness for the barbarians and
imitated their dress and accoutrements, seems to
have sought an interview with the Gothic king, and
suggested to him that instead of undertaking a hopeless siege he would do well to turn his steps southwards, where he would reap abundance of spoil from
the still undevastated plains of Greece. Alaric accepted the suggestion, and marched through Macedonia into Thessaly. There, however, his course
was stayed for a while by the arrival of Stilicho,
who, loyally fulfilling the behest of the dying Theodosius, had come with an army to deliver the in-
vaded Empire from its foe. Before manœuvres had *Stilicho*
forbidden
ceased and hard fighting had begun, there came a *to repel the*
strange, and at first sight incomprehensible, message *invasion.*
from the Eastern Court: 'Let Stilicho withdraw the
legions of Honorius within the limits of his master's

Empire, and let the legions of the East be sent to their proper quarters at Constantinople.' Loyally, but sadly, Stilicho obeyed the command, and thus the campaign of 395 closed, leaving Alaric in undisputed possession of the Greek peninsula. No Leonidas with his Three Hundred defended now Thermopylae, not even the easily held Isthmus of Corinth

Alaric in Greece.

was occupied by troops. All over the sacred places of Grecian story, Delphi, Corinth, Argos, Sparta, the tall barbarians swarmed. Only Athens seems to have escaped comparatively unharmed, a deliverance which the heathen historian[1] attributes to the fact that when Alaric approached the city he saw Athene Promachus, in such guise as she is represented in her statue, going round about its towers, and Achilles, the hero, such as Homer painted him in his wrath for the death of Patroclus, standing before the walls. Those who doubt the truth of these apparitions may accept the theory that the Acropolis was too strong to be taken, and that Alaric, who was no mere barbarous destroyer, was induced, partly by a heavy ransom and partly by reverence for her old renown, to refrain from sacking a city which was illustrious and venerable rather than wealthy or strategically important.

March of the recalled troops to Constantinople.

Meanwhile the troops which had been ordered to Constantinople, and which were commanded by Gainas the Goth, had done a strange and fearful deed. They loved Stilicho, and cursed the order issued by the officials at Constantinople which

[1] Zosimus v. 6.

parted them from his standards. Everywhere, as
they marched through the Empire they heard exe-
crations against the avarice and arrogance of the
Gaulish upstart, who presumed, forsooth, to put
himself forward as a suitable colleague for the Emperor. And, most important of all, their leader,
Gainas the Goth, aspired to play at Constantinople
the same part which Stilicho the Vandal was playing
at Milan. The soldiers said to one another that
when Rufinus met them at Constantinople he should
have a reception that he little expected.

When they reached the Capital they were drawn *The re-*
up in a great plain near the city, and Arcadius, with *view.*
Rufinus by his side, came thither to review them.
The two stood upon a high platform, conspicuous to
all, and those who were nearest could see Rufinus
plucking the Emperor's mantle and evidently de-
siring him to fulfil some promise which he had made
and to utter some oration to the army. In this
oration, could it have been delivered, the simple-
minded Arcadius, who would have done anything
which his minister commanded, was to have presented Rufinus to the army as his colleague in the
Empire. Then, had the programme been fulfilled,
the soldiers would have clashed their swords upon
their shields and shouted 'Ave Imperator': the
minister would have come forward and offered them
a liberal donative, and Rufinus Augustus would
have struck his coins commemorating his Justice,
his Temperance, and the Concord of the Emperors.

Such was the programme of the day's proceedings, *Death of*
Rufinus.

395.

but what actually occurred was very different from this. While the promised oration was still lingering on the lips of the scared and helpless Emperor, the army stretched forth both its wings and folded the high tribunal in a narrower and ever narrower embrace. Threatening gestures were made, and murmurs, not of acclamation, were heard. Soon the dreadful truth flashed upon Rufinus that he was surrounded, not by friends eager to be his subjects, but by enemies thirsting for his blood. A soldier stepped forth from the ranks, and mounting the platform, thrust him through with his sword, saying, 'With this sword Stilicho strikes thee.' Then the barbarians and the barbarised Roman soldiers carried the head of Rufinus round the city on a pole, strewed his limbs in fragments over the fields, and showed to every passer-by the dead hand opening and closing upon imaginary coins, while his mock courtiers shouted 'Give, give to the Insatiable.'

Even the heavy soul of Arcadius must have felt some stirrings of horror and resentment at such a tragedy enacted in his own sacred presence, but he passed at once under the dominion of other masters whose fortunes we cannot here follow. Gainas the Goth, Eutropius the Eunuch, Eudoxia the beautiful Empress, daughter of the Frankish general Bauto, kept up a vivid game of Court intrigue, and disputed with varying success for the chief place in that empty chamber which represented the mind of the Emperor.

We return to Alaric and his invasion of the Pelo-

ponnesus. Any dreams which he may have nourished 396.
of establishing his kingdom by the banks of the *Second campaign*
Eurotas or Cephissus were dispelled by the second *of Stilicho*
appearance of Stilicho, who, this time apparently at *against*
the earnest request of Arcadius, brought the army of *Alaric,*
Honorius for the deliverance of Greece. No great 396.
battle was fought, but Stilicho, who was evidently a
great master of strategy, penned up his antagonist in
the valleys of Arcadia. From this difficult position,
however, he allowed him to escape, whether through
mere carelessness, through fear of driving a powerful
foe to despair, by a tacit agreement that if liberated
he should at once evacuate Greece, or from what
other motive it is impossible now to say. The
enemies of Stilicho always asserted that both on this
and other occasions he refrained from crushing
Alaric when he had the power to do so, in order
that he, as the only general who could successfully
cope with him, might never find his services super-
fluous.

On evacuating Greece, Alaric with his Goths did *Alaric as*
not relapse into the position of a Fritigern or an *Roman governor of*
Athanaric. Another plan for the future had now *Illyricum.*
opened itself before him. As the time was not yet
come for conquering kingdoms he would accept once
more, in seeming, the position of a captain of *foederati*, but in such circumstances as to be still practically independent of the Empire. The part of the
Prefecture of Illyricum which had fallen to the
share of Arcadius consisted in its northern portion
of the so-called Diocese of Dacia, nearly correspond-

ing to the present kingdoms of Servia and Bosnia. Over this eastern Illyricum Alaric was placed as governor by the ministers of Arcadius. The precise official title which he bore is not mentioned. He may have been *Vicarius Daciae* or *Dux Daciae et Moesiae Primae:* but his power is undoubted. For the next four or five years he wielded all the enormous powers, both civil and military, of a Roman Imperial governor. He enlisted recruits, he managed arsenals, he collected taxes, though what proportion of the taxes so collected found its way into the Treasury of Byzantium no historian has told us.

Advantages of this position.

The especial advantage to Alaric of his position in this corner of Illyricum was that it enabled him to profit to the full by the discord existing between the two sections of the Empire, and at his pleasure to threaten either. He could with almost equal ease move southwards upon Macedon and Thrace and threaten Constantinople, or north-westwards to the Julian Alps, and so descend into Italy. This advantage is emphatically alluded to by a contemporary poet[1], who represents Stilicho as saying of him—

> ' Discord 'twixt East and West and mutual wrong,
> Not his own strength, has shielded him so long ;
> While he, deceitful, pledged his faith to both,
> And sold to each by turns his perjured oath.'

Yet doubtless during these years of repose his thoughts were turning with increased frequency to the West rather than to the East. He knew, none

[1] Claudian, De Bello Getico 565-7.

better, the matchless strength of the situation of
Constantinople. He suspected, if he did not know,
the comparative weakness of Rome. Moesia and
Thrace had been wandered over for years by the
wasting bands of his countrymen, while Italy, so
long the wealthy mistress of the world, was still un-
ravaged. Above all he had already begun to hear a
voice—like that which other makers of history, beings
such as Mohammed, Joan of Arc, Savonarola listened
to—telling them of great deeds set before them which
they should one day accomplish. And this voice—
call it by what name we may, it is vouched for by
contemporary evidence *before* its prediction was accomplished—said ever in his ears, 'Alaric, delay not.
Thou shalt penetrate to the City'[1]—the awful and
still inviolate majesty of Rome.

At length in the year 400 the thunder-cloud burst. *Alaric's*
Alaric, with the whole nation which obeyed him, the *first inva-*
sion of
women and children in the great Gothic waggons, *Italy,*
the warriors on their war-horses, moved slowly up *400-403.*
the valley of the Save, crossed the Julian Alps, and
by the way which he had learned when he rode in
the train of Theodosius, descended upon Italy. At
the same time, there is reason to think, another troop
of Goths, possibly belonging to the Ostrogothic section of the people, entered Italy under the leadership
of Radagaisus, but of their movements we have no
information, and even the fact of their invasion is
not generally admitted by historians.

[1] ' Rumpe omnes, Alarice, moras. Hoc impiger anno
   Alpibus Italiae ruptis, *penetrabis ad Urbem.*'
                     Claudian, De Bello Getico, 545-6.

400–402.   Of the three or four years (400–403) that Alaric spent in Italy during this invasion, we have the slenderest and most tantalisingly imperfect information from our authorities. We can say certainly that he did not reach Rome, probably did not cross the Apennines. There are dim rumours of a battle, a Roman defeat, somewhere near Aquileia. Then there is an inexplicable delay. During the whole of the year 401 Alaric appears to linger in Venetia and the valley of the Po, while Stilicho is fighting with some enemies (possibly Radagaisus and his Ostrogoths) in Raetia, and drawing in troops from the Rhine, and even from Britain, for the defence of the menaced capital. It was at this time that the Twentieth Legion was withdrawn from the cantonments which it had for centuries occupied at Chester, but to which it never returned.

Honorius retires to Ravenna.   The Emperor Honorius seems to have been besieged by Alaric either at Milan or the not distant city of Asta. If thus menaced, he at any rate sustained no actual injury; but the shock to his Imperial nerves of seeing the yellow-haired barbarians under the walls of his city had been so severe that he migrated to Ravenna, which strong city, effectually sheltered from every land-attack by the network of rivers and canals which surrounded *402–752.*   it, was from henceforth for three centuries and a half the regular residence of Roman Emperors, Ostrogothic Kings, and Byzantine Exarchs.

Battle of Pollentia.   At last, at Eastertide in the year 402, the armies of Stilicho and Alaric met in battle at Pollentia, a city of what is now Piedmont, about twenty miles *402–403.* south-east of Turin. The accounts of the battle are very conflicting, but it was probably a defeat, though not a decisive defeat, of the Goths. The advantage was gained by a piece of sharp practice which was hardly worthy of the troops of a Christian Emperor. It was Good Friday, and Alaric—an Arian, but a *4 Apr. 402.* zealous Christian—was celebrating the great event of Calvary in the usual manner, and not dreaming of battles, when one of Stilicho's officers, an Alan and a heathen, named Saulus, led an impetuous charge of cavalry against the Gothic army, and compelled it to turn from prayer to fighting. Saulus himself fell at the very beginning of the engagement, and the cavalry wavered ; but Stilicho and the legions of the centre restored the battle, and, perhaps, won the victory. But that the barbarian should have been forced against his will to fight on the most solemn fast-day of the Christian calendar was accounted a blot on the fair fame of Stilicho, and was not forgotten when the day of reckoning came between him and his enemies at the Imperial Court.

Another defeat, a doubtful defeat, of the Goths at *Alaric re-* Verona seems to have ended the war. In the year *tires from* *Italy, 403.* 403 Alaric made his way back out of Italy, probably over the Brenner Pass. He had not this time 'penetrated to the City' : he had lost some of his treasure, the spoils of preceding years, and, according to one account, his wife even had fallen into the enemy's hands. In itself the expedition had proved fruitless and inglorious enough, but it was the parent of mighty results; for doubtless in consequence of the withdrawal of the Imperial forces from the Rhine, a multitude of barbarous hordes—Vandals, Alans, and Suevi—poured from Germany into Gaul, and that fair province, the keystone of the arch of the Western Prefecture, was henceforward virtually lost to the Empire.

406.

Invasion of Radagaisus, 405.

Two years after Alaric's departure from Italy, his confederate Radagaisus returned to it, having 200,000 Goths (probably Ostrogoths) in his train. This man was spoken of with terror as 'by far the most savage of all the ancient or modern enemies of Rome.' He was a Pagan, and a rumour was spread abroad that he had vowed to offer to his country's savage gods the blood of the whole Roman people as an acceptable drink-offering. The impending heathenism without gave a despairing courage to the yet unsubdued heathenism within. The little knot of senators and their clients who still adhered to the ancient faith (which died out more slowly in Rome than anywhere else) dared to lift up their voices and openly assert that all these troubles were coming upon the State because she had left her old moorings, and because Jupiter Capitolinus and his family of gods were no longer receiving their ancient honours. However, there was not time for this party to effect a religious counter-revolution before deliverance came. If Radagaisus actually appeared under the walls of the City (which is doubtful), he soon departed and marched northwards into the rich land of Etruria. 405. Stilicho followed him with an army, in which Uldin the Hun and Sarus the Goth were conspicuous figures. Once again he played that clever strategic game which he had probably learnt from Theodosius, and which he had already twice successfully practised against Alaric in Greece and in Italy. He 'shut him up,' we are told, in that circle of *Radagaisus shut up near Fiesole.* mountains which surrounds Fiesole and looks down on Florence. Skilfully-posted detachments of troops prevented the savage invaders from piercing at any point through the iron girdle that encompassed them ; and this result being satisfactorily attained, of course the hugeness of the host only hastened the inevitable surrender. While the wild horde of Ostrogoths were starving in famished Fiesole, the soldiers of Stilicho were living in comfort—feasting, gaming, singing their rough camp-songs—but a sufficient number of them ever watching that none of the barbarians should creep over the mountains and escape. Before long the end came. Radagaisus, trying to steal forth by himself from the trap into which he and his followers had fallen, stumbled upon one of Stilicho's outposts, was brought before his conqueror, and, after a few days' interval, was put to death. The multitude which had accompanied *Radagaisus slain and his army sold into slavery.* him into Italy, with proud dreams of conquest and plunder, surrendering themselves at last to their watchful enemies, were all sold as slaves. So glutted was the market by their numbers that thousands of them fetched no more than an *aureus*

405.

(twelve shillings) apiece. But so long had the brave Teutons delayed their surrender, that even the food which their new masters gave them came, in the majority of cases, too late to save their lives; and the greedy purchaser found in thousands of instances that his *aureus* procured for him only the obligation to bury a starved-out Ostrogoth.

Nature of the manœuvre by which Radagaisus was defeated.

The fact that both Theodosius and the captain who had been formed in his school practised so often and so triumphantly this manœuvre of 'shutting up' the Goths suggests a question as to the reason of its success. We must remember that the armies which followed Fritigern, Alaric, and Radagaisus were, for the most part, *nation-armies*, encumbered with women and children, old men and other non-combatants, for whose conveyance a long train of waggons was needed. The Goths had no doubt some horses, since we hear of their cavalry, but they do not seem to have been essentially an equestrian nation; and their cavalry evidently lacked rapidity and nimbleness of movement, which was the cause of their defeat by the Huns.

So long as they could confine themselves to the great plains of the Danube and the Po, the overpowering numbers of this human torrent made them terrible and victorious; and even the waggons were useful, since when formed in square they made a rough but safe encampment. But when the time came for this nation-army to penetrate from one river-system to another, to cross the soaring range of the Balkans or the Apennines, then their difficulties

began.   Their deficiency of light cavalry prevented
them from reconnoitring well their ground, and ob-
taining (in those mapless days) the much-needed
information as to the easiest passes and the most
fruitful valleys.   Soon there would be stragglers
from the main host, and then petty and harassing
skirmishes to defend those stragglers.   The great
cumbrous waggons would stick in morasses.   There
would be night-alarms, and in the stampede of
cattle and flying men, many would be dashed down
precipitous ravines or swallowed up in swollen rivers.
By gentle but judicious pressure the Imperial general
would succeed in forcing the unwieldy procession
into some bay among the mountains carefully selected
beforehand, whence exit for heavily armed warriors,
for horses and for waggons was only possible by two
or three well-defined passes.   Then, if he could only
keep strict watch enough, his task was accomplished.
He would station his bravest soldiers, Huns very
likely, or even Gothic *foederati* on whose fidelity he
could depend, at the mouths of these passes, and
wait for hunger to do its swift work upon the cattle,
upon the little children, upon the women ; till at
length thousands of brave men who longed for
nothing so much as the opportunity to die fighting,
found even this denied them, and had to surrender
themselves and be sold as slaves to cultivate the lands
of some Roman lord whose dainty life one blow from
a Gothic fist would have at once annihilated.

This picture is chiefly an imaginary one [1], but those

_____
[1] Partly founded, however, on the experience of Theodoric in

†

408.

who remember the terrible scenes which marked the destruction of the British army in the Khyber Pass will, I think, recognise its probable truth.

We pass over three years and come to 408. Honorius, who was aged twenty-three, had now been for thirteen years the nominal ruler of the West. During the whole of that time the administration of affairs and the supreme command of armies had been in the hands of Stilicho, who, notwithstanding some blunders and some crimes, had upon the whole proved himself equal to the Herculean task which the weight of the falling Empire had brought upon him, and had certainly by his military genius marked himself out as the only champion fit to contend successfully with Alaric. This champion, through a sinister combination of fatuity, intolerance, and spite, was now struck down by the Emperor himself.

Revolt of Constantine in Britain, 407.

The circumstances of the Empire were more than ever difficult and perplexing. The usual British pretender to the purple had appeared in the shape of a private soldier named Constantine, whom (chiefly on account of his distinguished name) the legions still remaining in Britain had hailed as Imperator, and under whose command they had crossed over into Gaul to contend for such fragments of that wealthy province as still remained Roman, amid the generally pervading swarm of Franks, Vandals, Alans, and Alamanni. In the East the relations with Arcadius had been growing steadily worse for years. The present subject of contention was a

Thrace as described by Malchus. (See Italy and her Invaders, Book IV. cap. 3.)

claim—a preposterous claim as it seems to me— 408.
on the part of the Western Empire for the possession
of the whole instead of a mere half of the Prefecture
of Illyricum.   In support of this claim Alaric, who
seems to have been in frequent, almost confidential,
communication with Stilicho ever since his last *Negotia-*
invasion of Italy, had been engaged by that minister *tions*
to commence a joint invasion of the Eastern Empire. *between*
The project was, however, abandoned owing to the *Stilicho*
persuasions of Serena, the wife of Stilicho, who *and Alaric.*
appears in all good faith to have exerted her influence
with her husband and her Imperial cousins in order
to prevent the outbreak of war between Arcadius
and Honorius.   But Alaric, dissatisfied with such a
termination of the affair which left him and his
followers without their stipulated guerdon, suddenly
appeared at Aemona (Laybach) in a threatening
attitude, and demanded compensation for the trouble
and expense to which he had been put in preparing
for the abandoned expedition.

This extraordinary claim was brought by Stilicho *Alaric's*
before the Senate at Rome, and was supported by *claim for*
his own voice and by an easily procured letter from *compensa-*
Honorius.   Against such powerful advocates who *tion.*
could plead ?   The Conscript Fathers decided that
4000 pounds weight of gold (£160,000 sterling)
should be paid over to Alaric in consideration of his
not making war on either portion of the Empire.
One Senator alone, a man of high rank named
Lampadius, uttered an indignant exclamation[1], 'This

---

[1] 'Non est ista pax, sed pactio servitutis.'

408.

is no peace, but a selling of ourselves into slavery';
but fearing punishment for his boldness, when the
Senate was broken up he took refuge in a neighbouring church, the sanctity of whose asylum seems
to have preserved him from punishment [1].

*Danger of
Stilicho's
position.*

It might seem that a minister who could thus im-
pose his will on Emperor and Senate could do anything, but in fact the position of Stilicho was already
undermined.   His daughter Maria, wife of the
Emperor, had died, and the docile Honorius had
acquiesced in the command to marry her sister
Thermantia ; but it seems possible to discern in his
feeble soul some faint struggles of revolt against the
yoke which the Stilichonian family, especially his
mother-in-law, Serena, imposed upon him.   In the
legions, the regular Roman part of the army, there
was an increasing feeling of bitterness against the
favours shown, doubtless deservedly, to the Teutonic
foederati.   'Count Stilicho,' they said one to another,
'is after all a Vandal by birth, Sarus is a Goth,
Uldin is a Hun.   All the high commands are being
monopolised by men whose fathers were skin-clothed
barbarians.   We are Romans, the sons of the comrades of Romulus, scions of the race that has conquered the world, yet we are nothing in our own land.'
Side by side with this military discontent, there was
also ecclesiastical dissatisfaction.   Stilicho, if not
actually an Arian, pretty certainly threw his influence
into the scale against the persecuting edicts and civil
disabilities which the orthodox party were endeavour-

[1] He was Praefectus Praetorio under Attalus, 409.

ing to persuade the Emperor to hurl at the heretics. 408.
A rumour was also spread abroad—the truth or the
origin of which it is impossible now to ascertain—
that his son Eucherius shared that devotion to the
old idolatry which, as has been said, lingered on so
long among the nobility of Rome. Whatever the
truth of that rumour may have been, another report
which was industriously brought under the notice of
Honorius, that Stilicho was scheming to secure the
diadem for his son, was almost certainly unfounded.
In point of fact the great minister had shown singular
moderation in reference to the advancement of this
son, who at this time held only the unimportant
office of *Tribunus Notariorum.*

Such was already the thunderous state of the at- *Death of*
mosphere of the Court when news reached Ravenna *Arcadius,*
of the death of the Eastern Emperor, Arcadius. Both *1 May,* 408.
Honorius and Stilicho seem to have desired the
office of guardian to the young Theodosius, son of
Arcadius, and to have proposed to go to Constantinople to claim it. Stilicho had not much difficulty
in dissuading the timid and parsimonious Honorius
from the dangers and expense of the journey, but he
could not allay the suspicions which his own eagerness for the office had excited, that he was again
striving in an underhand way to procure either the
Eastern or the Western diadem for the young Pagan,
Eucherius. There was a certain officer of the Imperial guard named Olympius, 'a man who, under
the guise of devotion to Christianity, concealed every
kind of wickedness,' who was perpetually whispering

408.
Honorius in the camp at Tici- num.

into the Emperor's ear the danger to religion from this ambition of Stilicho. A camp had been formed at Ticinum (Pavia), for the soldiers who were to march into Gaul to quell the revolt of Constantine. To this camp, which seems to have contained a large preponderance of Roman-born soldiers, Honorius set forth accompanied by Olympius; and Stilicho, who had thus allowed his most useful instrument to be purloined from him, lingered in a curious state of irresolution and inactivity with his *foederati* round

Mutiny at Ticinum.

him at Bologna. Soon the news came of a terrible mutiny of the troops at Ticinum. Olympius had been ingratiating himself with the soldiers in every pos- sible way, visiting those who were sick, and on every occasion letting fall words of sympathy for · their hardships, and indignation at the partiality which constantly postponed their interests to those of the barbarian favourites of Stilicho. These hints, coming from an officer of the Imperial guard and a manifest favourite of the Emperor, had produced their na- tural effect. There had been what in Spanish politics is called a *pronunciamento.* The soldiers had risen in rebellion, slain four officers of the highest rank in the army and four heads of departments in the State, put the magistrates to flight, and held a carnival of blood in the city, robbing and murdering at their will.

At first the news ran that Honorius himself had been killed in the tumult, and then the *foederati* at Bo- logna urged, and Stilicho consented, that they should at once march to Ticinum and avenge his death. Soon, however, a correcter version of the affair was re-

ceived. Honorius was not dead, but had been paraded 408.
up and down the streets of the city by Olympius, in
a short military cloak and without a diadem, endea-
vouring to persuade the soldiers to return to their
obedience. In this he had at length succeeded. The
mutiny had been quelled, but the authors of it had
gained their end. All the more powerful friends
of Stilicho at Ticinum had been treacherously slain,
and it was now deemed safe to issue an order for the
apprehension of Stilicho himself. The officers of
the *foederati*, when the designs of the Court were
apparent, naturally wished to defend themselves and
their great general by force, but he refused to take
any part in such a civil war, 'not deeming it honourable or safe to employ barbarians against the Roman
army[1].' Sarus, the Goth, having no sympathy with
such scruples, perceiving that it would, in these circumstances, ruin his prospects of a military career
to be known as an adherent of Stilicho, ungenerously
turned against his old chief, slew the brave Huns
who formed his body-guard, and would fain have
captured Stilicho himself, who, however, fled to
Ravenna, but even in the hurry of his own flight
found time to warn the neighbouring cities not to
receive the *foederati* within their walls. Soon after
his arrival came a messenger from Olympius bearing
the Emperor's orders that he was to be apprehended
and imprisoned. Stilicho took refuge in one of the
many churches of Ravenna, but on the soldiers
swearing a solemn oath in the presence of the Bishop

[1] Zosimus v. 33.

that they were ordered to imprison him only but not to kill him, he surrendered himself to them. At once the same messenger produced a second letter from the Emperor, denouncing against Stilicho the punishment of death for his crimes against the Commonwealth. His friends and servants and a mass of indignant *foederati* entreated to be allowed to defend him by arms, but Stilicho sternly forbade them, and calmly presented his neck to the sword of the executioner (Aug. 22, 408).

Some men who have led apparently righteous and honourable lives are unmasked by Death, who exposes their well-hidden wickedness. In Stilicho's case Death wrought exactly the opposite change. At every step of his career we ask ourselves the question, 'Self-seeker or Patriot?' and it must be confessed that we scarcely get a perfectly satisfactory answer. But the closing scenes of his life show that he was indeed true to Rome, and refused the vengeance and the deliverance which lay all ready to his hand rather than use against her the swords of the barbarians.

The death of Stilicho was the signal for an outburst of jealous rage against his family and friends. Eucherius, who had fled to Rome, was before long put to death. Thermantia was sent back by Honorius to her mother. The adherents of Stilicho were tortured to make them confess his traitorous designs, and when they steadfastly denied the existence of any such, were beaten to death with cudgels. Above all, the Roman soldiers, in every city where the wives and children of the *foederati* were dwelling, rose in riotous insurrection, killing some and plundering others. Henceforth, of course, there was open war between legionaries and *foederati*, the latter of whom, to the number of 30,000, streamed forth to Alaric's Illyrian camp and urged him to avenge them on their cruel and cowardly foes.

408.

Mindful of his former reverses in Italy, Alaric, though the voice ' Penetrabis ad Urbem' was still ringing in his ears, offered peace to Honorius in exchange for a small sum of money, hostages, and the province of Pannonia, on which by this time the Empire can have had but a slender hold. Honorius, safe behind the canals of Ravenna, and relying on the prayers of Olympius, refused all terms of compromise, and late in this eventful year, 408, Alaric marched for the last time over the Julian Alps into Italy, never again to leave that land, the goal of so many aspirations. The events of the three years, 408–410, in each of which there was a siege of Rome, cannot here be related with any detail, and some of them are among the best-known commonplaces of history. I will only briefly assign to each year its distinguishing features.

Alaric invades Italy, 408.

The first, 408, was the year of *ransom*. Alaric, as has been said, in the later months of the year marched into Italy, and did not, as before, linger in the plains of Lombardy, but struck southward through Picenum and Umbria, marching no doubt by the great Flaminian Way, and stood before long at the gates of Rome. There seems to have been no opposition

Rome ransomed, 408.

to his progress. The 'Roman' party, so zealous in killing women and children and in organising *pronunciamentos*, slunk into their holes when an army appeared. It is probable that in this Italian expedition Alaric had made his host more of an army and less of a nation than on the previous occasion. We hear nothing of the waggons, and some of his marches and counter-marches can hardly have been performed with a long train of non-combatants following him.

At Alaric's appearance under their walls the Senate (for Honorius was safe at Ravenna) could think of no other means of opposing him than putting the hapless Serena, the widow of Stilicho, to death, fearing that she might open treacherous communications with the besiegers. The cowardly deed was not long unpunished. Alaric watched the Tiber above and below, and drew a strict line of blockade round the city. Hunger and pestilence were soon raging among the people, and the Senate found itself compelled to send ambassadors to Alaric to ask his terms. The threat that despair might drive the citizens to some audacious sortie was met by the well-known answer, 'The thicker the hay, the easier mown': the enquiry what Alaric meant to leave them if he insisted on their surrendering all their gold, all their moveable property, and all their barbarian slaves, by the equally well-known words, 'Your lives [1].'

More days of famine followed. At length a final

[1] Or 'your souls.'

embassy arranged the terms of the ransom which 408. Alaric condescended to receive from the Imperial City. It consisted of 5000 lbs. weight of gold (£225,000), 30,000 lbs. of silver (£90,000), 4000 silken tunics, 3000 scarlet hides, and 3000 lbs. of pepper. The date of this transaction is not known, but it was probably in the very last days of 408.

The next year, 409, is the *year of the anti-Emperor, Attalus.* All Alaric's dealings with the Senate and People of Rome at this time were directed to the conclusion of a firm treaty of alliance, offensive and defensive, with the Emperor. His aim was not to conquer Rome, or to settle his followers in any part of Italy, but to legitimise his position within the Empire, to have a large space on the Middle Danube, either Noricum or Pannonia, assigned to his people, and then to be recognised as Rome's champion against all other enemies. In fact, he desired to renew the old *federate* relation only on a footing of equality instead of one of semi-dependence. To all such propositions Honorius, or rather the ministers who spoke in his name, replied with an unceasing '*non possumus*,' as they could not be attacked, being safe behind the dykes and lagoons of Ravenna. Alaric's only resource was to put pressure, even cruel pressure, on Rome, in order to bring her sovereign to terms.

409. Alaric negotiates Moderation of his requests.

A considerable part of the year 409 was consumed in these vain negotiations. The Praetorian Prefect, Jovius, who had supplanted Olympius in the position of chief adviser of the Emperor, seems to have

Oath sworn by the head of Honorius.

409.

been at first disposed to try to make terms with Alaric, and to see if the title '*Magister Utriusque Militiae*' could not divert him from his schemes of conquest. But Honorius demurred to the proposal, and Jovius, accommodating himself to his master's humour, insisted on all the chief officers of the Emperor assembling round him and swearing by their master's head (which they touched in making the asseveration) that they would make no peace with Alaric, but would wage against him perpetual war. To all subsequent overtures of Alaric (and some of them surprise us by their moderation, offering terms such as the Empire might have safely and honourably granted), this tremendous oath by the empty head of Honorius was opposed as an insuperable obstacle.

Attalus proclaimed Emperor.

Alaric, whose patience was worn out, returned to Rome, and again formed the blockade of the City. But the Senate, whose patience was equally exhausted, refused to again undergo the horrors of famine and pestilence for the ungrateful Honorius, and sent messengers to Alaric declaring that they were willing to renounce their allegiance to the Emperor. Peace on these terms was easily arranged. Attalus, the Praetorian Prefect of the City, a man of Greek extraction, was saluted as Emperor, and in that capacity concluded a treaty with Alaric, recognising him as an ally of the Empire, probably conceding to him a settlement in the coveted provinces on the Danube, and conferring on him at once the splendid position of *Magister Utriusque Militiae.*

So opened the year 410, the ever-memorable year
of the *Third Siege and Capture of Rome*.   It seemed
for a time as if Attalus would indeed wrest the Rule
of All Things from his incapable rival.   He marched
towards Ravenna, from whence issued forth a piteous
supplication for peace on the basis of a yet further
subdivided Empire.   If Honorius might but continue
to reign at Ravenna, Attalus should reign at Rome,
and the *Concordia Augustorum* might unite them
and Constantine, the Emperor of the Gauls, with
the son of Arcadius, Emperor of the East.   Attalus
made a cruel and insulting reply, threatening his
rival with mutilation and banishment : but the timely
arrival at Ravenna of six legions from Constantinople prevented him from carrying his threat into
execution, and turned the tide of fortune.   Famine
again threatened Rome, from another cause than
the blockade of Alaric.   Heraclian, to whom had
been entrusted the execution of the sentence against
Stilicho, was now holding the great province of Africa
loyally for Honorius, and by cutting off the food
supplies of Carthage from Rome, brought the City
into such terrible straits that an angry cry was heard
in the Amphitheatre, when the new Emperor was
sitting there in state watching the games, ' Pone
pretium carni humanae ' (' Fix the tariff for human
flesh ').   Alaric's keen eye saw that Africa was now
the key of the position, and he urged upon Attalus
the necessity of sending troops, barbarian *foederati*,
thither to overcome Heraclian.   But Attalus, who
was evidently a futile, inefficient ruler, delayed and

410.
Attalus
refuses to
divide Italy
with Ho-
norius.

Supplies
from
Africa
stopped.

410.

lingered, and, as it was hinted, began to entertain schemes for disembarrassing himself of the oppressive patronage of the Visigoth. At length Alaric, tired of his vacillation and bad faith, and recognising the failure of his scheme of creating a rival Emperor, assembled his army on the plain outside Ariminum, and there, in the sight of thousands of Romans and Goths, formally stripped Attalus of the emblems of Empire, and proclaimed that he was reduced to the rank of a private citizen.

Attalus deposed.

The diadem and the purple were sent to Honorius at Ravenna, and it seemed for a moment as if the just and honourable peace, so eagerly desired by Italy, by Rome, and by Alaric, might be secured. But Sarus the Goth, the same man who had turned treacherously against Stilicho in his adversity, and who, perhaps on that account, hated Alaric and was hated by him, entered Ravenna at the head of 300 veterans, and succeeded in breaking off the just-resumed thread of the negotiations.

Sarus breaks off the negotiations between Alaric and Honorius.

Then at length, as it seemed that nothing but the sword could cut the Gordian knot, Alaric again crossed the Apennines, determined to show what he could do to Rome as an enemy, since she in her infatuation rejected him as a friend.

Alaric enters Rome, 24 Aug. 410.

There was this time no long agony of blockade, no famine or pestilence. On the night of the 24th of August, 410, almost as soon as he had appeared under the walls of the City, Alaric effected an entrance through the Salarian Gate, at the north-east corner of the City, at very nearly the same place where, on the

20th Sept. 1870, the soldiers of Victor Emmanuel 410. entered Rome. Whether the gate was carried by a sudden surprise, or was opened by slaves or treacherous citizens within, it is impossible now to decide; but the theory of surprise seems, upon the whole, most probable. The splendid palace of the historian Sallust, hard by the Salarian Gate, was set on fire, and its spacious gardens had their beauty ruined by the entering Gothic soldiers.

Thus, then, at length 'the great city which reigned *Rome* over the kings of the whole earth' was captured and *sacked.* was pillaged by a foreign and a barbarian enemy. Civil war, sedition, frenzied Emperors had 'dealt upon the Seven-hilled City's pride' in the course of the centuries; but not for 800 years—not since Brennus and his Gauls had slain the Conscript Fathers in the Forum—had Rome been violently entered by a conquering foreign foe. There were some alleviations to the horrors of the capture, derived from the fact that the assailants were Christians; and these alleviations are naturally emphasised by the Church historians, from whom we derive most of our scanty information as to the Third Siege of Rome. Alaric had ordered that no Christian church should be injured, and that the right of asylum, especially in the two great Basilicas of St. Peter and St. Paul, should be religiously observed. These orders were perhaps made known to the citizens, multitudes of whom, Pagan as well as Christian, were soon flying for shelter to these islands of safety. But notwithstanding any such humane orders, honourable both to the general who issued them and to the army by whom they were obeyed, the sack of a great and wealthy city by a hungry and exasperated army of barbarians was of necessity a terrible thing. We hear of an aged widow beaten to death to make her disclose her imaginary treasures, of matrons ravished, of palaces laid in ashes. And above all rose now the terrible fact that *Roma Invicta* had been conquered. Where one barbarian chief had penetrated, more could, and of a surety would, follow. The citizens henceforth—like men who have lived through a great and fearful earthquake—must live evermore in dread of seeing the ghastly terror recommence.

As even political caricatures may sometimes help us to understand what contemporary spectators think of the actors on the stage of history, let us listen to Procopius, who wrote 150 years later, but who has preserved to us a possibly contemporary story, as to the reception of the news of the fall of Rome by the Roman Augustus.

Reception of the tidings by Honorius.

'They say that at Ravenna one of the eunuchs who was in charge of the Imperial poultry announced to the Emperor Honorius that Roma had actually perished. Whereupon he cried with a loud voice—"But just now he fed out of my hands!" [for he had an exceedingly large fowl, Roma, by name.] Then the eunuch, understanding what was passing in his mind, said that it was Roma the *City* which had been destroyed by Alaric. But the Emperor in reply said, "But I thought, my friend, that

the *bird* Roma had perished!"—so great they say 410.
was the stupidity of this Emperor.'

The capture of Rome by Alaric, though an event *The cap-*
of incalculable importance in the history of the world, *ture of*
settled nothing in the immediate present. Still the *settled*
Augustus, the only legitimate source of power in the *nothing.*
Roman State, remained inaccessible at Ravenna.
Still Heraclian, his yet loyal governor of Africa,
held that province for his master, withholding the
grain-supplies without which Rome could not live.
Still Alaric could not conquer that firm peace,
guaranteed by sufficient hostages, and securing to
him a lawful position in the Empire, without which
he was determined not to return to Illyricum. He
marched to the extreme south of Italy, and designed
to cross over into Sicily, in whose ports he would probably have collected an armament for the conquest
of Africa. But he never effected the passage of the
Straits of Messina, the ships which he had collected
at Rhegium being destroyed by a violent storm.
While he was still lingering in Calabria he was *Death of*
seized by an illness, which lasted but a few days. *Alaric,*
He had 'penetrated to the City'; his work was *410.*
done. The fateful voice rang in his ears no longer,
telling him of great exploits yet reserved for him in
the future, but instead of it came Death. He was
probably in about the forty-fifth year of his age; so
that he, like Theodosius, left great possibilities of
conquest unexhausted. But in his short career he
had done enough to change the current of the
world's history.

410.
Burial of Alaric.

The story of his burial is well known. In order to guard his grave from the possibility of insult at the hands of the Provincials, a number of captives were employed in diverting the stream of the Busentus, a river of Bruttii. In the old river-bed a great trench was dug, wherein were laid the bones of the conquering king, and, after the fashion of his heathen forefathers, some of the most precious spoils of Rome were laid by his side, that he might not miss them in the gardens of Paradise or the halls of Walhalla. Then the trench was filled in, the river was turned back into its ancient bed, the captives were slain : and thus 'no man knoweth his sepulchre unto this day.'

LECTURE VI.

PLACIDIA: ATTILA.

AN interval of forty-two years elapsed between *Historical perspective.* Alaric's sack of Rome and the next great barbarian invasion of Italy. To us, looking at these years as they appear on the outstretched map of History, it is manifest that they were years of gradual but progressive decline and decay for the Roman Empire. Probably, but not certainly, they wore the same aspect to contemporary observers. But the important point to remember is that there *was* such an interval between the first and the second acts of the great World-Tragedy. Reading history in a manual, or glancing over it in such a rapid sketch as I am now attempting to draw, we are apt to forget how slowly some of its scenes have unrolled themselves. Superficial students, if they do not actually confound Alaric with Attila, often think of them as contemporaries, perhaps as allies, and suppose that they and Genseric and Odoacer, by some combined and concerted effort, brought about 'the fall of the Western Empire.' What I want to impress upon my hearers is the fact that if a child was born on the day that Alaric was laid under the waters of the 410. Busentus, he would be a middle-aged man when Attila 452.

stood under the walls of Aquileia, and would be verg-
ing on threescore and ten when the last Roman
Emperor of the West was bidden to hand over the
purple and the diadem to a barbarian conqueror. I
ask also for a full measure of pity for those true
Roman hearts whose allotted span of life had to be
all passed in these years of irresistible decline.
There are times like that of which a poet has sung—

> ' Bliss was it in those days to be alive,
>   And to be young was very heaven ; '

times like the first years that followed the battle of
Salamis, like the first thrill and rapture of the
Crusades, like 'the spacious days of great Elizabeth,'
when the life of a nation has been so strong, so fresh,
and so triumphant that one feels as if even the
saddest individual life must have been overflowed by
the great national gladness and saved from utter
sorrow. On the other hand, could even the most un-
clouded domestic happiness atone to a patriotic
Roman who lived in the fifth century for the necessity
of watching the lingering agony of his country ? Like
a man dwelling upon a subsiding continent, he saw
one familiar landmark after another submerged beneath the waters of barbarism. Or like those remote
descendants of ours, if such shall then be living on this
planet, who, as physical philosophers tell us, will see
this earth begin to part with her atmosphere and
become incapable of sustaining organic life, he must
have felt that all the old conditions of being were in-
verted, and that life by the beautiful Mediterranean
was going to become in truth unliveable.

In order to bring the length of this interval of comparative tranquillity properly before our minds, let us
trace the fortunes of one person who lived through it,
a daughter, sister, wife and mother of Emperors, the
lady Galla Placidia.   The daughter of Theodosius's *Early life*
second marriage, she lost her mother, Galla, when *of Placidia, born about*
a child of five or six years old, and her father in the 388.
following year.   She appears to have been brought *Death of*
up at Rome, perhaps by her kinswoman Serena, *Galla, 394. Death of*
who possibly intended that she should be the bride *Theodo-*
of her son, Eucherius.   Her position was one of for- *sius, 395.*
lorn splendour, that of an orphan with no sister and
with two such brothers as Arcadius and Honorius ;
nor does it appear to have been cheered by any
gleams of friendship between herself and the house
of Stilicho.   When Alaric first appeared under the
walls of Rome, the resolution to put Serena to death
as his suspected accomplice was taken 'by the
Senate and by the Emperor's sister, Placidia[1].'
Probably the name of a young maiden of twenty was
somewhat ostentatiously used by the Senate in order
to justify their own action against the niece of the
great Theodosius : still it is impossible for the
admirers of Placidia (of whom I am one) not to
regret that her influence on this occasion was
exerted on the side of vengeance rather than on the
side of compassion.   It was probably at the end of *Captivity*
the first siege of Rome that Placidia was taken *of Placidia.*
prisoner by the Goths, who retained her as a hostage,
but treated her with all outward show of honour and

[1] Zosimus v. 38.

royal ministrations. She was therefore doubtless present at the great assembly at Ariminum, where her brother's rival, Attalus, was deposed; she would hear from the Gothic soldiers their histories of the sack of Rome; she perhaps saw the mighty form of her conqueror outstretched in death in his tent by the Busentus. Now, for the next five years, her history was to be singularly interwoven with that of his brother-in-law and successor, Ataulfus.

Alaric's successor, Ataulfus.

This man, whose name is in fact the same as one of those borne by another great Northern conqueror, Gustavus *Adolphus*, had joined Alaric with reinforcements raised in Upper Pannonia in the year 409, and had taken part in the skirmishes with Sarus before Ravenna, which preceded the Third Siege of Rome. He was a blood-relation [1] of Alaric, as well as his kinsman by marriage, and was by general acclamation hailed as his successor and raised on the shield as king. Though not boasting the full number of inches of a Gothic warrior, he was of shapely form and noble countenance. He is especially interesting to us, because a chance conversation with a Provincial, a conversation which passed at Narbonne and was reported at Bethlehem, gives us a glimpse into his own secret hopes and aspirations, such as we do not possess into the mind of any other leader of the barbarians. Orosius tells us that when he was at Bethlehem he heard a citizen of Narbonne, who had served under Theodosius, and who was a wise and religious person, say that

---

[1] ' Consanguineo,' Jord. xxx.

Ataulfus had frequently told him 'that his first thought when he entered on the career of conquest had been to claim for the Goths all that leadership of the world which had once belonged to the Romans, and to vindicate for himself a position like that which had belonged to the mighty Augustus. Gradually, however, the fashion of his dreams had changed. He saw that it was not by the sword alone, but by law, that Rome had dominated the world, and that his own countrymen, wild and impetuous, had not learned that lesson of obedience to Law which alone could fit them to rule ; and now his whole desire was to restore and re-invigorate the great Roman Commonwealth, transforming that which he once hoped to destroy.'

Consciously or unconsciously every really statesmanlike intellect among the Northern chieftains must have gone through the same change and come to the same conclusion.   Out of the Goth, or the Frank, or the Saxon alone it was not possible yet to form a law-abiding nation.   Either from the Roman State or the Roman Church they must learn those habits of discipline and self-restraint which they did in the end learn, and practise as no purely Romance nation, far less any purely Celtic nation, has ever practised them.   What Ataulfus saw to be the statesman's true aim was that which Theodoric accomplished with temporary, and Charlemagne with somewhat more permanent success—that transfusion of fresh Teutonic blood into the old Roman body which has in fact made modern Europe.

*Loves of
Ataulfus
and Pla-
cidia.*

The political conversion of Ataulfus was aided, as conversions have been so often aided, by a woman. The fair Placidia, forced to follow all the movements of the Gothic army, yet 'treated with all honour and ever tended with royal ministrations,' vanquished his heart. The old saying that 'conquered Greece led her victor captive' was renewed with Placidia and Ataulfus; but with a delicacy which we should term chivalrous if we were speaking of a later age, he refused to make her his bride, though she too loved him, till the consent of her brother came from Ravenna. After four years of weary negotiations this consent was obtained, but not until the Goths had marched out of Italy into

*Their mar-
riage at
Narbonne,
414.*

Gaul. In January, 414, the marriage of the Gothic king and the Roman Lady was celebrated at Narbonne at the house of a citizen named Ingenuus. The 'wise and religious person' who afterwards conversed with Jerome at Bethlehem was doubtless present at the wedding, if indeed he were not (as is very probable) Ingenuus himself. Men noticed with interest that Ataulfus entered the inner apartment to claim his bride, dressed, not in the barbaric splendour of his countrymen, but like a Roman Senator. They saw with admiration the fifty goodly youths in silken robes, bearing plates filled with gold and gems, who formed part of Ataulfus' splendid *Morgen-gabe*[1] to his bride. Then came music, and they saw, perhaps not without a touch of scorn, Attalus, once Emperor of Rome, leading the dance and song in honour of his great patron's wedding.

[1] Morning-gift.

Unhappily for the world, this union of Roman and *Fortunes of the Visigothic kingdom.* barbarian led to no abiding results. The kingdom set up by Ataulfus did indeed endure, though not exactly in the shape which he had given to it. Established at first chiefly as a South Gaulish kingdom, and remaining such till the conquests of Clovis at the end of the fifth century, it then shifted its centre of gravity southward of the Pyrenees and became that Visigothic kingdom of Spain which was overthrown by the Moors in 711, and which gradually crept back to life again under the kings of Leon, Castille, and Arragon. But the dynasty of Ataulfus himself was short-lived. A child, named Theodosius, was born to him by Placidia ; but this child, around which so many hopes *Death of Placidia's child,* centered, died, to the unspeakable grief of its parents, and was buried in a silver coffin at Barcelona, *and of* where they then dwelt. Soon after the infant's *Ataulfus,* death the father was stabbed in the back by one *415.* of his servants, who thus avenged an old grudge for the execution of a former master. His dying words to his brother were, ' Live in peace with Rome and restore Placidia to Honorius.'

The murder of Ataulfus was possibly connected *Humiliations of Placidia.* with a sort of insurrection against the Roman influences which had been of late so powerful in the Gothic Court. His successor, the brutal Singeric, murdered the sons of Ataulfus (the children of his first marriage) and forced Placidia to walk as a captive before his chariot for twelve miles from the gates of Barcelona. After only eight days' reign

416–423. however, this ruffian was dethroned and slain, and the gallant Walia was acclaimed king, whose name is one of the most distinguished in the early history of the Visigothic monarchy.   He renewed and *She is re-* strengthened the alliance with Rome, and gave *stored to* back Placidia to the Emperor, receiving in return *Honorius,* the somewhat prosaic ransom of 19,000 quarters of *416.* corn.

Her mar- Placidia was escorted by the Roman general who *riage to* had received her from the hands of the Goths to *Constan-* her brother's Court at Ravenna, and there, nearly *tius.* two years after the death of Ataulfus, she gave her hand to this general, an old lover of hers named Constantius.

Second The union of Constantius and Placidia lasted four *widowhood* years, and the fruit of it was a son and a daughter, *and exile of* years, and the fruit of it was a son and a daughter, *Placidia.* the first named Valentinian (after his maternal great-grandfather), the second, Honoria. Constantius, a brave soldier, but a rough, sullen, unpopular man, was associated in the Empire by his brother-in-law, and, after six months' enjoyment of the Imperial dignity, died, apparently of mere *ennui,* in 421. Two years after his death, Placidia and her children withdrew to Constantinople, on account of a quarrel which had broken out with her brother, who, as I suspect from the description of his conduct, had begun to show symptoms of softening of the brain.

Death of In this same year (423) Honorius died at the age *Honorius.* of thirty-nine, and was buried in a gigantic marble sarcophagus, which may still be seen in 'the Mauso-leum of Galla Placidia' at Ravenna.   There was no

member of the family of Theodosius on the spot to
claim the vacant diadem, and Joannes, a somewhat
obscure member of the Civil Service (*Primicerius
Notariorum*), was permitted to wear it, under the
patronage of the powerful *Magister Militum*, Castinus.

423–425.
*Elevation
of Joannes.*

When the news of this event (usurpation we must
not call it, for there was no strict hereditary right in
the Roman Empire) reached the Court of Constantinople, the young Emperor Theodosius II, the son
of Arcadius, determined to send an expedition to the
West to overthrow Joannes. The expedition was
commanded by two brave Alans—father and son—
named Ardaburius and Aspar ; and, after one or
two reverses, was in the end completely successful.
Joannes was brought as a prisoner to Aquileia ; his
right hand was cut off, he was paraded round the
city upon an ass, and, after some more ungenerous
insults of this kind, he was put to death. Ravenna,
which had sympathised with the elevation of Joannes,
was punished by being sacked by the soldiers of
Ardaburius. Rome was flattered by the young
Valentinian III, a boy of seven years old, being sent
there to assume the purple. At Constantinople,
Theodosius II and his people, who were assembled
in the Hippodrome when the news of victory arrived, walked in procession to the great Basilica,
singing praises to God for his deliverance.

*Theodosius
II places
the son of
Placidia on
the West-
ern throne.*

From 425 to 450, that is, from the thirty-eighth to
the sixty-third year of her life, Placidia was virtually
the sovereign of what remained of the Western

*Placidia as
regent,*
425–450.

425–450. Empire. She was already styled Augusta in right of her husband Constantius' six months' wearing of the purple. She was, in accordance with one or two precedents, entitled to hold the reins of power (with the rank, though not the precise title, of Regent) during her son's minority: and as that son was idle and pleasure-loving, reproducing only the weaker features of the Theodosian character, she continued to hold them after he had grown to manhood, and until her own death in 450.

Events of Placidia's regency.

Great events, disastrous events, were happening during this second quarter of the fifth century. In the Church of the East the wind was rising for that great storm of the Monophysite controversy which for a hundred years took peace from the earth. In the West, Carthage was being conquered by the Vandals, Gaul and Spain were being more and more hopelessly lost to the Empire, 'the groans of the Britons' were being borne across the sea to 'Aetius, thrice Consul.' All these events Placidia had to witness with failing heart from her palace at Ravenna by the Pine Wood and the sea.

Her chief adviser, Aetius.

If the Augusta did not herself display any conspicuous faculty of rule during these twenty-five years of decline, she at least had the merit of loyally supporting the one man who, like Stilicho in the previous generation, was best able to sustain the falling Empire. This was that 'Aetius thrice Consul' to whom allusion has just been made. He was born at Silistria, on the Danube, the son of Gaudentius, an official of high rank in the Western Empire.

If he was not of barbarian extraction, a point on 425–450.
which we cannot speak with certainty, the events of
his life threw him into close intercourse with the
barbarians.   For three years a hostage in the camp
of the Visigoths, and then, for an indefinite time,
hostage in the country of the Huns, he had con-
tracted friendships with the leading men of both
nations, had perhaps learned something of their
language, had doubtless observed their tactics and
formed his own opinion of the best means of defeat-
ing them [1]. After the death of Honorius he had
adhered to the party of Joannes, but, not having
been able to avert his overthrow, he had accepted
high command under Placidia and Valentinian, whom
he served loyally to the end of his days [2].   Loyally,
that is, as far as his sovereigns were concerned.   If
the hitherto accepted story of his quarrel with Bonifacius, governor of Africa, be correct, there was
deep disloyalty on the part of Aetius towards his
greatest colleague in the Imperial service, and that
disloyalty cost a province to the Empire; but the
account of these transactions may be reserved till
the next lecture, in which I shall have to speak of
the conquests of the Vandals.   During ten years,
from 429 to 439, the energies of Aetius were chiefly
directed to maintaining some hold on the East and
Centre of Gaul, with which object he waged war with
diverse success on the Visigoths, the Franks, and

---

[1] In several points of his military career, Aetius seems to me
a not unworthy precursor of Belisarius.

[2] With a short interval of exile in Hunland, 433.

the Burgundians, and it is noteworthy that in these wars the most useful auxiliaries of Aetius were men of the Hunnish nation.   During the last nine years

Danger from the Huns.

of the life of Placidia (441–450) the chief factor in European politics, the care that bit most deeply into the hearts both of the Eastern and Western Sovereigns of the Empire, was the menacing might of ATTILA, king of the HUNS.   To these savage Asiatic marauders it is now time to turn our attention.

History of the Huns after 374.

For more than fifty years after the Huns crossed the Sea of Azof, and fell like a thunderbolt on the kingdom of Hermanric the Ostrogoth, their history is almost a blank.   They had set in motion an avalanche of ruin on the Empire, but they themselves, though doubtless spreading wide the terror of their name through Southern Russia and Hungary, and though once travelling southward as far as Antioch on a marauding expedition, did not often during this period come forward as claimants for the goods of the dying Empire.   In fact, as we have already seen, on several occasions the Hunnish soldier seems to have been the bravest and most faithful of the auxiliaries of Rome.   In part this was probably due to common enmity to the intervening Visigoths.   The Roman Provincial hated and feared the Goth : the Goth feared and loathed the Hun : accordingly the Roman and the Hun found it for their interest to be friends.

Attila's accession, 433.

In the year 433, Attila and his brother Bleda mounted the throne of the Huns.   Twelve years later Bleda died, having been, according to some accounts, craftily slain by order of his brother.   At

all times Attila's was the commanding personality, 433.
and with him alone need we here concern ourselves.
Let us hear how he is described by the historian of
the Goths[1] : 'Attila was a man born into the world *His cha-*
to agitate the nations, the fear of all lands, one who, *racter and*
I hardly know how, terrified all by the awful appre- *ance.*
hensions spread abroad concerning him. He was
proud in his gait, rolling his eyes hither and thither,
so that the elation of his heart showed itself even by
every movement of his body : a lover of war, but not
himself given to acts of violence[2], mighty in counsel,
placable by those who humbled themselves before
him, favourable to those whom he had admitted to
his fealty : short of stature, broad of chest, with an
over-large head, with little eyes, thin beard, hair
sprinkled with grey, turned-up nose, muddy complexion. All these were the characteristics which
recalled his origin' [or, to use our modern phrase-
ology, the distinctive marks of the Mongol race].
' By natural temperament he was always con-
fident that he should do great things, but this confidence of his was increased by finding "the sword *The sword*
of Mars," which is ever held sacred by the Scythian *of Mars.*
kings, and which is said to have been discovered in
this way. A certain herdsman saw one of his heifers
limping, and being anxious to discover the cause of
her wound, carefully followed her bleeding footprints
through the grass, till at length he came to the sword,
upon which the heifer had incautiously trodden while

---

[1] Jordanes xxxv.

[2] ' Bellorum quidem amator, sed ipse manu temperans.'

433-441.   grazing, and having dug it up he at once carried it to Attila. He, having gratified the herdsman with a generous present, deemed himself to be now appointed sovereign of the whole world, and victory in all wars to be assured to him in right of the sword of Mars.'

433.
Hunnish demands at Constantinople.

Immediately upon the accession of Attila and Bleda, they demanded and obtained from the Eastern Emperor the duplication of their yearly *stipendium*, or, as they more truly called it, tribute, which was now raised from £14,000 to £28,000. At the same time they insisted on the return of all Huns or Romans who had fled from the Hunnish dominions and taken refuge under the ineffectual aegis of Rome. This demand for the surrender of refugees, the result, doubtless, of the barbarous despotism of the Huns, was afterwards frequently renewed, and its imperfect fulfilment was a standing grievance against the Eastern Emperor.

433-441.
Extent of Attila's Empire.

For the next eight years, however, we hear but little of diplomatic relations between Attila and the Empire. There can be little doubt that during these years he was engaged in consolidating his dominions northwards and eastwards. His own peculiar territory was evidently the flat land of what we now call Hungary, between the Danube and the Carpathians ; but the nations which owned his over-lordship stretched probably from the Caspian to the Rhine. Very loose and ill-compacted, no doubt, was the Empire of the Huns; but the kings of the Ostrogoths, Gepidae, Alans, Suevi, and Heruli, all followed Attila to battle, all formed part of that con- *433-441.* federacy of rapine which he could hurl whenever it pleased him against a civilised and wealthy foe.

In the East another Tartar horde, the Geougen, *His cam-* perhaps even more savage than the Huns them- *paigns in Asia.* selves, threatened the new barbarian Empire; but Attila appears to have formed an alliance with China which neutralised their hostility, and left him free to prosecute his designs of conquest west of the Ural mountains and south of the Caspian. He marched from the latter sea fifteen days southward into the Persian kingdom, and ravaged the ancient province of Media. He evidently ruled without a rival in European Russia, or at least in that part of it which was then worthy of even a barbarian's notice, and— what is more important to us—he had, we are told, 'subjected the islands in the ocean to his sway.' These 'islands in the ocean' can be none other than *Did he* the islands and peninsula of Denmark and the *drive our* southern part of Sweden, which the geographers of *Saxon forefathers* the time considered to be an island. Now, however *from their* transient may have been the Hunnish conquest of *homes?* those Baltic lands, of Holstein, Jutland, and South Sweden, it was sufficient to produce results of world-historical importance. In those lands our fathers, the Saxons, the Jutes, the Angles, were dwelling at the commencement of the fifth century, making doubtless many a piratical raid against the '*Litus Saxonicum*' in Britain, but, as a rule, returning with their plunder to their homes by the Baltic. From those lands, before the year 441, they had begun to swarm forth, alighting upon the eastern and southern coasts of Britain, coming probably with wives and children, and coming to conquer and to *remain*. Why this new and sudden change in the current of the nation's thoughts? Surely it was the swarthy Hunnish riders, the same who had scared the Visigoths across the Danube, who sent the Angle and the Saxon in their long ships scudding across the German Ocean. If this be so, the obscure movements of this squalid Hunnish people not only threw down the Empire of Rome, but indirectly caused the building up of the Empire of England.

Attila tor-ments the Eastern and West-ern Courts with his embassies, 441-450. With the year 441, Attila re-enters the arena of Imperial politics. For the next nine years he sends ceaseless embassies to the Eastern and Western Empires, ostensibly to press for the redress of grievances, really in order to claim higher and ever higher terms for the maintenance of peace, and to enrich his favourites at Court by the presents which he well knows that the trembling Augusti at Constantinople and Ravenna will give them in order to purchase their good offices with their master.

The standing grievance against the Eastern Court was, as has been said, the alleged failure to surrender the fugitives, Hunnish princes or Roman merchants, who had escaped from Attila's dominions. The chief grievances against Placidia and Valentinian were two : the vases of Sirmium and the dowry of the lady Honoria.

(1) A certain Gaulish provincial named Constantius, who filled the post of Secretary to Attila,

when the city of Sirmium was besieged by the Huns,
received from the Bishop of that city a deposit of the *The matter of the Sirmian vases.*
rich gold Communion-plate of the Church, in trust to
apply the proceeds to the ransoming of the Bishop
and his flock. Regardless, however, of this trust,
he carried off the sacred vessels to Rome and raised a
large sum of money upon them from the goldsmith,
Silvanus. Eventually Sirmium was taken ; Constantius, a traitor to all parties, was crucified ; and
Attila, claiming a sort of 'resulting trust' of the
vases for himself as conqueror, insisted that Silvanus
should be surrendered to him as having stolen *his*
property.

(2) Honoria, the sister of Valentinian III, a *Honoria's ring.*
young and giddy girl, had compromised her reputation by an intrigue with an Imperial chamberlain,
and was sent by her mother to the Court of Constantinople in a kind of honourable imprisonment.
Her spirit chafed at the seclusion in which she was
kept by her four middle-aged and almost nun-like
cousins, and she formed the wild scheme of plighting
her troth to the King of the Huns, and calling upon
him to be her deliverer. Attila received the ring
which she sent him, and, though he had already
many wives, disdained not to add Honoria to the
number, so far at least as this that 'he claimed as
her betrothed husband one half of the Western
Empire which had been bequeathed to Honoria by
her father, but out of which she was kept by her
brother's covetousness.'

The most important of the return-embassies was

Embassy of that which was sent by Theodosius II, in the year
448. 448, to the Court of Attila. The chief ambassador
was Maximin, a man of illustrious birth and high
official rank ; and the official whom we should call the
Secretary of Legation was Priscus, to whose able
pen we owe a minute account of the embassy, which
is certainly the most interesting historical document
of the century. Both Maximin and Priscus were
Pagans, and both were men of high character.

Imperial They were used, however, to cloak an infamous plot
plot for which had been concerted at the Court of Con-
Attila's stantinople, but of which they were themselves
assassina- ignorant, for the assassination of Attila by one of the
tion. nobles of his guard named Edeco. It is like reading
a chapter of *Quentin Durward* or *Les Trois
Mousquetaires*, to see the way in which the plot is
hatched, developed, and finally detected : and the
honest indignation of Attila against 'his slave,
Theodosius, who paid him tribute but dared to plot
the 'assassination of his master,' is finely expressed,
and puts the savage Hun for the time immeasurably
above the cultured and nominally Christian Emperor.
I have no space here, however, to insert these details ;
but, though it has been often quoted before, I must
transcribe Priscus's account of Attila's palace and of a
banquet therein, to which he and his chief were invited.

Attila's 'Having crossed some more rivers we arrived at
palace. length at a very large village, in which was situated
the palace of Attila. This dwelling was, we were
told, the finest building in all the country. It was
made of logs and smooth planks, and surrounded by

wooden palisades, not for safety but for ornament. 448.
Next to the King's house, that of Onegesius (his
chief minister) was most conspicuous. It, too, was
surrounded by a palisading, but was not adorned
with towers as Attila's was. Not far from this enclosure was a bath which Onegesius had built of
stones brought from Pannonian quarries, for the barbarians who dwell there have not a stick nor a stone
in their own country, but have to import all building
materials from a distance. The architect of this
bath was carried captive from Sirmium, and hoped
to receive his freedom as the reward of his ingenuity;
but unconsciously he prepared for himself a worse
lot than that of ordinary slavery, for Onegesius made
him his bath-man, and he had to wait upon him and
his retinue whenever they had a mind to bathe.'

The Banquet.

'When we returned to our tent, there came an *Attila's banquet.*
invitation to us both from Attila to be present at his
banquet, which would take place about 3 P.M. Punc-
tually, at the time appointed, we went to the dinner
and stood on the threshold before Attila. According
to the custom of the country, the cup-bearer brought
us a bowl of wine that we might pray for the good-
luck of the host before taking our seats. When this
was done, and we had just tasted the bowl, we came
to the chairs of state on which we were to sit at
dinner-time. All the seats of the guests were ranged
along the walls on either side of the building. In the
centre of all sat Attila on a couch, with another couch

behind him, behind which again a flight of steps led
up to his bed, hidden by curtains of white linen and
variegated stuffs, ornamentally arranged as the
Greeks and Romans prepare the nuptial couch.'
Then the order of precedence is described. The
Ambassadors, to their evident surprise, found that
the seats of honour were given, not to them, but to
Hunnish nobles.

'Opposite to Onegesius on a double chair sat two
of the sons of Attila, while his eldest son sat on
Attila's couch, not near to him but on its extreme
verge, and with eyes cast down upon the ground
through awe of his father. When all were thus
arranged in order, the cup-bearer came in and
handed to Attila his ivy-wood drinking-cup filled
with wine. When he had received it, he saluted
him who sat nearest him in rank. The guest thus
honoured stood up, and it was not etiquette for him
to sit down till he had sipped or drunk off the wine
and returned the goblet to the cup-bearer. In the
same way all who were present showed their respect
to the King: he remaining seated all the while, they
stood up, received the cup, greeted him and tasted
the wine. Behind each guest stood a cup-bearer,
whose business it was to go into the centre of the
hall, each in his proper order, and meet Attila's cup-
bearer coming out from beside his master.

'Then entered first Attila's servant bearing a
plate full of meat, and after him came the general
waiters who laid bread and other victuals on the
tables, of which there was one for every three or

four guests, or sometimes more.   For all the rest of 448.
the barbarians and for us a costly banquet had been
prepared, which was served on silver dishes, but
Attila had plain meat on his wooden plate.   He
showed also simple tastes in all his other surround-
ings.   For the other banqueters had golden and
silver drinking-cups put beside them, but his was of
wood.   His raiment also was quite plain, distinguished by its cleanness only from that of any of his
followers; and neither the sword which was hung
up beside him, nor the clasps of his barbaresque
shoes, nor the bridle of his horse, was adorned, as
is the case with other Huns, with gold or precious
stones or anything else that is costly.'

Priscus then again describes the drinking of Attila's
health, which was performed by all the guests, standing, between each of the courses.

'When evening came on, torches were lighted, and
two barbarians coming in and standing opposite to
Attila, recited songs previously composed, in which
they sang of his victories and his warlike virtues.
The banqueters gazed earnestly on the minstrels;
some were delighted with the poems; others, remembering past conflicts, felt their souls stirred within
them; while the old were melted into tears by the
thought that their bodies were grown weak through
age and their hot hearts were compelled into repose.

'When the songs were ended a mad Hun came forward, who by his strange, wild, incessant chatter moved
all the guests to laughter.   After him entered Zercon

448.

the Moor' [whom we know from another source [1] to have been a hump-backed dwarf with ape-like nose]. 'By his garb, his voice, and his wild promiscuous jumble of Latin, Hunnish, and Gothic words, he sent all present, except Attila, into fits of laughter. The King, however, remained quite unmoved, changed not a line of his countenance, and neither by word nor deed showed the slightest enjoyment of the joke, except that when his youngest son, Ernak, came in and stood beside him he gently pinched his cheek and looked upon him with kindly gaze. When I expressed my wonder at his neglect of his other sons and the favour which he showed to this one, the barbarian who sat beside me and who understood the Italian language, after making me promise secrecy, assured me that the prophets had foretold to Attila that his race should suffer reverses and then be raised up again by this son.

'When we had sat at the banquet till far into the night, we departed, not wishing to persist in drinking any longer.'

From this single picture we may imagine the scenes which frequently occurred when the Ambassadors of Theodosius and Valentinian came, with fearful hearts, into the presence of Attila, striving, yet striving in vain, to keep up the traditions of the majesty of Rome. We may imagine, too, the reception which would be accorded to the Teutonic under-kings, Gepid, Herul, Ostrogoth, when they came, as assuredly they would come, at least

[1] Suidas.

once a year, into the presence of their supreme 450.
lord.

The years from 441 to 450, the era of embassies, *Deaths of*
came to an end. In 450 death wrought great changes *Placidia*
and Theo-
in the palaces both of Ravenna and Constantinople. *dosius II,*
In the West, Placidia died, and the functions as well 450.
as the show of governing had to be assumed by
Valentinian III, who still for a time gave his confidence loyally to Aetius. In the East, Theodosius II
died of injuries received by a fall from a runaway
horse, and the sovereign power became vested in his
sister Pulcheria and her husband, the brave old
soldier, Marcian. The next Ambassador sent by *Marcian,*
Marcian's orders to the Court of Attila took a higher *the new*
Eastern
and more manly tone than the Hun had heard during *Emperor,*
the whole reign of Theodosius. It was clear that *will not*
truckle to
there would be no more chance of sending oppres- *Attila.*
sive embassies, of doubling and quadrupling the
'tribute,' or of worrying about the return of refugees.
Any further advantages that were to be gained from
the East must be gained at the point of the sword:
and upon a survey of the whole situation, Attila
decided that since the time had come for war it
should be war, not with the East but with the West,
not with the grim Marcian but with the soft and
indolent Valentinian.

There is thus a certain correspondence between
the careers of Alaric and Attila. Each took up a
position on the confines of the two Empires. Each
at first spent some years in making war or threatening war on the Eastern Empire, and each finally

devoted his whole energies to war with the Empire of the West.

Attila prepares for war with the Western Empire.

Pretexts for war were of course easily found. The great question of the vases of Sirmium was probably still unsettled. Honoria's dowry had certainly not been handed over to the affianced Hun. Aetius, warring in Gaul, had seated on one of the Frankish thrones a young prince (possibly Meroveus), whose supplanted rival claimed the assistance of Attila. Above all, the Huns and their allies yearned to burn, to plunder, to slay, and the Western provinces alone could at the moment satiate this desire. Attila did not, however, entirely neglect the prudent precautions of a statesman. He concluded an alliance, offensive and defensive, with Gaiseric, the Vandal conqueror of Carthage, an alliance which, had it been followed up by a well-timed Vandal attack on Rome, might probably have ended the life of the Western Empire.

Alliance between that Empire and the Visigoths.

On the other hand, Aetius, at this crisis of the fortunes of Gaul, concluded an alliance which was of infinite importance, both for its immediate results and for the rearrangement of parties to which it pointed in the not distant future. Theodoric the Visigoth, successor of Walia, reigned at Toulouse over a well-compacted monarchy which had been rapidly growing in strength and in civilisation. We are now speaking of a time forty-one years after Alaric's sack of Rome : and the days when the Visigoths were a wandering horde of *foederati*, seeking on almost any terms for a recognised position within the Empire, are already far below the horizon. Theo-

doric is the acknowledged lord of one of the fairest 451.
portions of Gaul ; his people have become a domi-
nant caste of warriors, whose ascendancy the Provincials do not dream of disputing; but Aetius has
been for years struggling, sometimes with the aid of
Hunnish auxiliaries, to prevent him from extending
his dominion yet further over Gaul.

Now, in the presence of this vaster danger, this
thunder-cloud rolling up from the plains of Hungary,
which threatens to overwhelm Goth and Roman in
one common ruin, all these bickerings cease. The
Visigoth no doubt is yet barbarous, but he is rapidly
becoming civilised ; while the Hun is an utter
savage. The Visigoth, though an Arian, is a Christian ; the Hun is a brutal Pagan. The Visigoth desires, it is true, to rule in Gaul ; but the Hun will
utterly destroy it. The result of these considera-
tions was that Aetius and Theodoric formed an
alliance against the invader, and, notwithstanding
some delays and some misunderstandings, they
seem on the whole to have both honourably observed its obligations.

At Eastertide, 451, the waters of the great deep *Attila en-*
were broken up. The motley host, said to number *ters Gaul,*
half a million of men, marshalled by 'a mob of *451.*
kings[1],' but all trembling at the nod of Attila, moved
westward, hewed down trees in the Thuringer
Wald, and, on the rude boats and rafts which they
thus constructed, crossed the Rhine. All the towns

---

[1] 'Turba regum' (Jordanes xxxviii). Compare the story of
Talma playing to a *parquet* of Kings in the days of Napoleon.

451. in Belgic Gaul—Tongres, Metz, Rheims—yielded to their savage onslaught. Everywhere flew the red banner of fire. The citizens were slain on their hearth-stones; the priests, against whom the invaders had an especial hatred, were murdered before the altars, on which glittered the coveted silver and gold. Paris escaped destruction; whether saved by the prayers of Sainte Geneviève or guarded by its own comparative insignificance it is not for us to decide. So the savage host, having rolled on through Belgic and Lugdunensian Gaul, reached the great river Loire, which circled the kingdom of the

Siege of Orleans. Visigoths. Here they laid siege to Orleans, that city so memorable for her sieges. The battering-rams (for Attila possessed these engines of war) were shaking the walls of the city, and the inhabitants feared that only ruin was before them. But their Bishop, Anianus, bade them be of good courage, and foretold that deliverance would reach them on the 24th of June. On that day, while they were praying in the church, Anianus sent a messenger to mount the ramparts and see if help were approaching. The messenger went once, twice, in vain. The third time he brought word that a cloud of dust was seen upon the horizon. It was caused by the troops of Aetius and Theodoric, who, after some delay and wavering of purpose, had joined forces and were approaching to deliver the city. Attila, for some reason with which we are not acquainted, declined to await their attack, and began to retrace his steps towards the Rhine. Doubtless his vast

army was difficult to feed, and difficult to keep to- *451.*
gether, in the country which they had so ruthlessly
ravaged; and probably Attila foresaw great danger
in attempting to cross the broad Loire in the face
of a large army, which united Gothic courage to
Roman science of war. Whatever the cause, he *Attila*
retreated, and reached the city of Troyes, which he *retreats.*
consented to exempt from pillage on condition that
the Bishop, St. Lupus, whose saintly appearance
awed and impressed him, should accompany him as
far as the Rhine. On the Mauriac plain, some five
miles from Troyes, the pursuing armies came up
with him; and here was fought that 'cruel, mani-
fold, monstrous, and stubborn battle [1]' to which historians have given, not quite correctly, the name of
the Battle of Châlons.

Before the fight began, Attila consulted the rude *'Battle of*
auguries of his nation, drawn from the inspection of *Châlons.*
the bowels of a sheep and the markings of some *July? 451.*
bones. The soothsayers predicted 'ill fortune to
the Huns,' but qualified it with the assurance that
the leader of their foes should fall. The hope that
Aetius, the one great Roman champion, would perish,
seemed to console Attila for the presage of his own
defeat.

It was indeed a battle of many nations. Under
the standards of the king of the Huns marched
Ostrogoths, Gepidae, Heruli, and a host of less-
known nationalities, Teutonic, Slavonic, and Turanian. The three kings of the Ostrogoths, and

---

[1] 'Bellum atrox, multiplex, immane, pertinax.' Jordanes xl.

451.

especially the eldest of them, Walamir, and Ardaric, king of the Gepidae, were Attila's chief advisers and lieutenants on the battle-field.

The allied army, on the other hand, contained not only Visigoths, who were posted on the right wing, and Romans, who were on the left, but Franks, Saxons, Bretons, Burgundians, and a number of other tribes settled in Gaul. Chief among these lesser nationalities were the Alans, who were settled at Valence on the Rhone. They were near of kin to the Huns, and their king, Sangiban, was suspected of intending to desert to them on the battle-field. He was therefore placed in the centre of the allied line, tightly wedged in between Romans and Visigoths, both of whom watched his movements narrowly and prevented him from accomplishing the meditated treachery.

Beyond this statement as to the Alans, and Attila's orders to his troops to neglect the Romans and strike hardest at the Visigoths, we hear little or nothing as to the tactics of the day. The battle began at three in the afternoon, and raged on, upon a line of immense length, till the end of the July day. Theodoric, the Visigothic king, was thrown from his horse and accidentally trampled to death by his own *Hunnish* countrymen. His men, however, rushed forward *defeat.* and broke the Hunnish line. Attila himself fled and took shelter behind his rampart of waggons. Thorismund, son of Theodoric, and Aetius both lost their way in the darkness which had now come on, and nearly fell victims to their rashness,

having actually wandered into the quarters of the 451.
foe.

The next morning dawned upon a ghastly sight. *Results of*
It is said that 177,000 men were slain in the 'mani- *the battle.*
fold and monstrous battle.' This number represents
a slaughter nearly twice as great as that at Leipsic,
with all the improvements in the machinery of destruction which fifteen centuries have wrought. It
is doubtful whether we ought to listen with perfect
faith to calculations which were probably very hasty
and fragmentary. But it is not doubtful that the
slaughter on the Mauriac plain was one of the
greatest ever witnessed on any battle-field before the
invention of gunpowder. And, measured by its results, the battle was even greater than when we take
account of the carnage. For this was pre-eminently
one of 'the decisive battles of history,' since it
settled the question of supremacy in Europe against
the Hun, the squalid, unprogressive heathen Tartar,
and kept the ground clear for the Romance, the
Teutonic, and the Slavic peoples.

The expectations of both armies that the battle *Attila*
would be renewed on the morrow were not fulfilled. *retreats*
from Gaul.
Attila, behind his entrenchments, bade his trumpets
sound, and feigned a fresh attack, but all the time he
knew himself beaten, and had a pyre of Hunnish
saddles prepared, into which, had his entrenchments
been stormed, he would have cast himself headlong,
that living or dead he might escape the insults of
his foes. Meanwhile the Goths, having at length
found their old king's body, buried him on the battle-

451-2. field to the music of their rough war-songs. Thorismund then marched rapidly to Toulouse to claim his
father's throne. Aetius also quitted the field, and
Attila was saved from utter destruction, whether
owing to the too great prudence of the allies or to
a want of perfect harmony between them, it is
impossible now to determine. The Hunnish king
reached the Rhine without further molestation, and
thence sent the venerable Bishop Lupus back to
Troyes, asking him to pray to the Almighty for the
welfare of his late entertainer.

Attila's in-
vasion of
Italy, 452.
The next year (452) Attila determined to wipe out
the shame of his defeat by an invasion, not this time
of Gaul, but of Italy. He crossed the Julian Alps,
entered Venetia by the well-known route, trodden of
late by so many armies, and invested the great, the
Siege of
Aquileia.
hitherto impregnable city of Aquileia. In two stubborn
sieges at least, probably in more, this city had shown
herself the unconquerable bulwark of North-east
Italy ; and now, so long was the investment by the
Huns vainly protracted, that it seemed as if she
would once more prove her title to that name. Attila was about to abandon the siege in despair, when
suddenly looking up, he beheld the storks collecting
their young broods about them and preparing to
fly from the city. The omen struck him. He
pointed it out to his soldiers, and in a short, inspirit-
ing speech, urged them to renew their attack on
a city which, as the heaven-guided instinct of the
birds told them, was doomed to ruin. The appeal
was fatally successful. The fierce Huns once more

moved their engines against the walls; they effected a *452.*
practicable breach; they swarmed in; they slew, they
pillaged, they ravished. The rage of Attila at his *Aquileia*
long detention before the walls made the usual *taken and*
destroyed.
savagery of Tartar destruction more savage; and
soon there was nothing left of Aquileia—its Mint, its
Baths, its Theatres—but a smoking heap of ruins.
Tradition says that Attila caused a mound to be
raised at Udine, twenty miles distant, and stood on
the top of it to see the flames ascend from the
burning city.

All the sister cities, beautiful and stately, which *Other*
Adriatic
were mirrored in the waters of the North-western *cities*
Adriatic, shared the fate of Aquileia. The Roman *ruined.*
colony of Concordia; Altinum, with its fair white
villas; Patavium, the birthplace of Livy, were
levelled with the ground. A few trembling fugitives from all these cities, including, perhaps, some
from Aquileia herself, sought shelter in the wide
lagoons at the mouths of the Piave and the Brenta.
These miserable refugees founded a gorgeous city, *Founders*
whose fame spread far and wide over all lands, and *of Venice.*
whose merchandise was sold even on those dreary
plains of Central Asia over which Attila's ancestors
once wandered. She was the affianced City of the
Sea—Venice.

Attila marched westwards through the broad green *Attila at*
plain which we now call Lombardy, and as he went *Milan.*
his fury somewhat abated. All the cities, Verona,
Pavia, Milan, and the rest opened their gates to him;
and in all, the Huns plundered at their will, but the

452. lives of the inhabitants were spared and the buildings were left unburned. At Milan, Attila saw with contemptuous amusement a picture representing the Scythians prostrate under the feet of the Eastern and Western Emperors. He allowed the picture to remain, but ordered an artist to paint on the opposite wall the King of the Huns seated on his throne, with Theodosius and Valentinian emptying their sacks of *aurei* at his feet.

Embassy of Pope Leo.　　During all this time abject terror reigned in the City of Rome, where, and not at Ravenna, the Emperor appears to have been residing. Even the stout heart of Aetius seems to have failed him, and he is said to have counselled Valentinian to flee from Italy, probably to the Narbonensian Gaul, almost the only Western province which was left to Rome. However, it was decided to try what effect a humble embassy might have in mitigating the wrath of the terrible Hun. Two of the highest officials in the Empire were sent on this embassy, and with them went Pope Leo I, greatest in character and mental gifts of all the men who had yet sat in the chair of St. Peter, rightly named Leo, for a more lion-hearted man had not been found even among the Consuls and Emperors of Rome.

Its success.　　The embassy found the Hunnish king by the banks of the Mincio, probably not far from the city of Mantua. Strange to say, they won a peaceful and easy victory. '[1] He laid aside his fury and excitement, and returning by the way that he had come, that

[1] Jordanes.

is to say beyond the Danube, he departed with the 452.
promise of peace, uttering, however, this one warning
and threat above all others, that he would bring
yet heavier calamities upon Italy unless they sent to
him Honoria, with the portion of the Imperial
treasure which was her due.' We shall probably
seek in vain for any reasons of state-craft which
could have induced Attila thus to forego the supreme
prize of barbarian conquest, the sack of Rome, when
victory lay ready to his hand. Apparently the
reason assigned by contemporary chroniclers is the
true one. It was the influence exerted over him by
the saintly majesty of Leo, which induced him to
sheathe the sword and to be satisfied with promise
of tribute when he might have grasped the reality of
plunder. There was in Attila's character, with all
its brutal savageness, something almost like magnanimity, a certain readiness, when his own greatness
was acknowledged and when his enemy had humbled
himself in the dust before him, to accept his humiliation, and if he trampled, not to trample him to death.
There was also in his heathen soul some capacity of
being impressed by those whose spirits really rose
above the clash of the kingdoms of the world, into
the serener air of the Kingdom of God. There may
possibly have been mingled with this feeling a
remembrance of the premature death of Alaric which
followed so soon upon his conquest of the Eternal
City, and a fear that he too, if he sacked Rome,
might find his grave in Italy.

Whatever the cause, there can be no doubt that

452-4.   the success of Pope Leo, when the Emperor and the Master of the Soldiery confessed that they saw only ruin before them, profoundly stirred the hearts of the Roman people. The events of the year 452 contributed enormously to raise the Vatican above the Palatine, and to give the Pope the moral, if not yet the political, sovereignty of Rome.

Death of Attila, 453.   If Attila had planned for himself the luxury of another raid upon Italy in 453, his schemes were suddenly and unexpectedly frustrated. In addition to the many wives whom he already possessed, he married a beautiful damsel named Ildico. At the wedding banquet he drank copiously, and afterwards slept the sleep of intoxication. In the midst of it he was attacked by a violent bleeding from the nose, which proved fatal to him in his drunken stupor. That same night, it is said, the brave Emperor Marcian had a dream, in which he saw the bow of Attila broken.

The Hunnish power broken.   The great Hunnish king received a magnificent burial from his people. Three coffins, one of gold, one of silver, one of iron, enclosed his body, but the precise place of his burial was kept a secret. After his death the ascendancy which by his own tremendous force of character he had been able to exert over many subject nations, suddenly vanished. His sons proposed to partition his realm among themselves. The auxiliary peoples resented the proposal: the great confederacy was broken up: Ostrogoths, 454.   Gepidae, and Heruli met the young Hunnish kings in battle by the Pannonian river Netad. Attila's

sons were beaten, his first-born slain, the rest put 454.
to flight.   Ernak, his father's favourite, became a
subject-ally of the Eastern Emperor, and ruled at
the mouth of the Danube.

But the great Hunnish Empire after its short and
terrible day of dominion was now a thing of the past,
a vanished nightmare of the nations.   The fierce
Hun had himself built nothing that endured, though
indirectly he had contributed to three of the greatest
changes in Europe,—the 'making of England,' the
establishment of the Papal Supremacy, the foundation of Venice.

LECTURE VII.

Gaiseric.

We have seen that though the north-east corner of Italy was cruelly ravaged by the Huns, the Eternal City herself escaped the degradation of their presence as conquerors. But the blow, which had been averted by the embassy of Pope Leo, fell three years later (455), the agents of destruction being now, not the Huns, but the Vandals. I purposely abstained in my last lecture from making any but the slightest allusion to the Vandal conquest of Africa (428–439), though that was in fact one of the most important events under the government of Placidia, and certainly the event which produced the most permanently disastrous consequences for Rome.

Early history of the Vandals. If we go back from the fifth century after Christ to the first, we shall find that the Vandals were then dwelling not far from the Baltic coast in the countries which we now call West Prussia and Posen. A little later on, sharing the general southward movement of all these races, they appear in Silesia and give their name to the *Vandalici Montes*, which are the same that are now called Riesengebirge, the Mountains of the Giants. Possibly there may be in

the new name some dim remembrance of the old, for
we are told [1] that the Vandals, as well as the Gepidae,
were nearly allied in blood to the Goths, and like
them were tall of stature, fair-skinned, yellow-haired,
and handsome.

In the reign of Marcus Aurelius (171) we find
them in the plains of Hungary warring against the
Romans. Three years later they have become the
allies of Rome, and this attitude of friendship towards the Empire is generally maintained by them
for more than two centuries (174–406). Especially
was this the case in the latter part of the reign of
the Emperor Constantine (330), when the Vandals
had suffered a terrible and well-nigh exterminating
defeat at the hands of their Gothic kindred, by the
banks of the river Marisia. The survivors of that
terrible day humbly pleaded for permission to enter
the province of Pannonia on the western shore of
the Danube, and there to dwell as *foederati* under
the protection of the Empire. For more than sixty
years they faithfully observed this treaty. This was
probably the time in which they embraced the Christian faith under that Arian form of it which Ulfilas
had preached to the Goths. Many of their chiefs
doubtless entered the service of the Emperors as
life-guardsmen, and it was probably in this way that
the father of the great Stilicho, though a Vandal,
rose high enough to prepare a splendid position for
his son.

The calumniators of Stilicho attributed to him,

*The Van-
dals enter
Gaul,* 406.

---

[1] By Procopius, de Bello Vandal. i. 2.

406–409.   probably most unjustly, a share in the next development of Vandal history.   It came to pass in the year
406, in the interval of suspense between the first
and second invasions of Alaric, and just after the
exhausting campaign with the terrible Radagaisus,
that (as has been already mentioned) three great
barbarian hordes, taking advantage of the defence-
less state of the Rhine-frontier, denuded of its
legions for the defence of Italy, poured westwards
into the provinces of Gaul.   These three tribes were
the *Suevi,* a name of puzzling indefiniteness, once including almost all the High-German family of nations; the *Alans,* a Tartar horde who had come
into Europe at the same time as the Huns, but had
pressed further westwards than their kinsmen; and
the *Vandals.*

War with   If Stilicho had anything whatever to do with the
the Franks. invitation or the permission given to these barbarian
hordes to enter Gaul, it is probable [1] that he did it in
the hope of finding in them a counterpoise to the
Franks, who were already appearing with menacing
strength in the north-eastern provinces of that
country.   At any rate the Franks are the only enemy
that we hear of as attempting to bar their way.   A
great battle was fought, in which Godigisclus, the
Vandal king, fell with 20,000 of his followers, and
only the timely intervention of Respendial, King of
the Alans, saved the Vandals from utter destruction.

Three   Of the three years which followed (407–409) we
years of   know nothing, but must imagine the three con-
ravage,
407–409.   [1] As suggested by Papencordt, Geschichte der Vandalen, p. 339.

federated nations marching up and down in Gaul ^{407-409.}
during that period, slaying and plundering at their
will.   Then, by the internal discords of the Empire,
a fresh prospect of rapine was opened out before
them.   The British usurper, Constantine, who had
penetrated with his legions into Spain, found his
precarious throne undermined by one of his officers
named Gerontius, who proclaimed his son Maximus
Emperor.   While usurper and sub-usurper were
quarrelling, the defence of the Empire, which both
pretended to maintain, was neglected.   The passes
of the Pyrenees, which had hitherto been easily and 409.
faithfully guarded, were left open to the enemy, and
the three confederate nations marching through
them, found the rich and fruitful peninsula of Spain,
which had enjoyed four centuries of unbroken peace,
at their mercy.   The day of the month, even the day
of the week of this terrible invasion, was recorded by
the Spanish chroniclers, faithfully reproducing the
deep dint which it had made on the memories of
their countrymen.

'In this year' (409) 'the Alani and Wandali and *The Van-*
Suevi entered the provinces of Spain, on the 28th *dals and*
of September, on the third day of the week[1].'   After *federates*
wandering about for some time, enjoying the luxury *enter*
Spain, 28

¹ Idatius.   'Alani et Wandali et Suevi Hispanias ingressi : alii *Sept.* 409.
quarto Kalendas [28 Sept.], alii tertio Idus Octobris [13 Oct.] me-
morant die, tertiâ feriâ.'   Tillemont points out that the 28th September in that year fell on a Tuesday, but the 13th October on a
Wednesday.   Very likely the fifteen days' difference between the
two calculations denotes the interval between the passage of the van
and the rear of the invading host.

409-428.   of promiscuous pillage, they divided the country in
some rough fashion between them, the Suevi taking
to themselves Gallicia in the north-western corner of
Spain, the Alans, Lusitania on the west and the
province of Carthagena on the east.   The Vandals
were divided into two branches, the smaller of whom,
the Asdingi, dwelt in Gallicia near to the Suevi,
while the powerful clan of the Silingi occupied the
fertile province of Baetica in the south.   To these

413.   entered, four years after, the Visigoths under Ataulfus : and by these four, or if we choose so to consider them, five barbarian nations, as well as by the
Roman garrisons in the strong cities which remained
like islands amid the barbarian flood, the hapless provinces of Spain were ruled and plundered.   Famine
soon followed in the train of war.   Women were
accused of eating their own children : and some
Visigothic soldiers bought of some Vandals a small
mug-full of wheat for an aureus (=12 shillings).

Internecine   I need not trouble you with the details of the wars
war be-
tween the   which raged in Spain from 413 to 428.   The Visi-
barbarians goths were generally in alliance with the Empire,
in Spain,
413–428.   and fought their fellow-barbarians, especially the
Vandals, with whom they had a long-standing family
quarrel, with a ferocity which astonished the Romans.   First the Silingian Vandals in Baetica and
then the Alans sustained crushing defeats at their
hands : and the scanty remnants of these tribes
joined themselves to the Asdingian Vandals, who
under their king Gunderic, son of Godigisclus, had
now, from the most insignificant, become the most

powerful nation in the Peninsula, especially as the *420–427.*
Visigoths at this time seem tó have withdrawn most
of their men north of the Pyrenees, being intent on
building up their dominion in Southern Gaul.

In 420 the Asdingian Vandals, with their de- *The Van-*
pendents the Alans marched across Spain and took *dals occupy*
Andalusia,
up their quarters in the fertile Baetica, where their *420.*
kinsmen formerly dwelt. In 422, Gunderic won a
decisive victory over Castinus, the Roman Master
of the Soldiery, leaving 20,000 Imperial soldiers
dead upon the field. In 425 he took the great city
of Hispalis (Seville), and fitted out a naval expedition for the conquest of the Balearic Islands. In
427 Gunderic died,—'attacked by a demon,' says a *Death of*
Spanish chronicler, 'by the just judgment of God, *King Gun-*
deric, 427.
to punish him for having stretched forth his hand
against the Church of Seville,' and he was succeeded
by GAISERIC [1], the illegitimate son of his father Gode- *Accession*
gisclus. *of Gaiseric.*

Such was the position of affairs in Spain when a *Gaiseric*
messenger came from Bonifacius, Count of Africa, *invited by*
Count
inviting the Vandals to cross the sea and wrest that *Bonifacius*
province from the Empire. The cause of this strange *to enter*
Africa,
proposition is fully told us by one historian [2], writing *427.*
a hundred years after the event, and though accurate
and trustworthy for his own times, very apt to con-
fuse persons and places of which he had no personal

[1] Often called Genseric by modern historians, but there is no doubt
that Gaiseric is the more correct form of the name, and it is the one
now generally adopted by German scholars.

[2] Procopius.

427.

knowledge. His narrative has been lately subjected
to a severe analysis by a great master of historical
criticism[1], who has shown how many questionable
elements it contains. Still, in the absence of all
other information, it holds the field, and I will therefore, with this caution, tell the story in the words of
Procopius himself.

*Procopius's
story of the
rivalry
between
Aetius and
Bonifacius.*

'The calamity of Africa came to pass in this fashion.
There were two Roman generals, Aetius and Bonifacius, both able men, and in knowledge of the art of
war second to none of their time.   Between these
men jealousies arose as to the government of the
Empire : but so great were their magnanimity and
other virtues that if any one were to call each of
them the last of the Romans he would not be far
from the truth, so completely had all the glory of
Rome become merged in these two men.   One of
these two men, Bonifacius, Placidia set over the
whole of Africa, hereby offending Aetius, who, however, did not show his displeasure, for the ill-feeling
between them had not yet produced an open rupture,
but was hidden under the mask of friendship.

'Now when Bonifacius had departed for Africa,
Aetius began to calumniate him to Placidia as a man
who aspired to the Imperial dignity and would wrest
Africa from her and the Emperor.   He assured her
that it would not be difficult to bring this matter
to the test, for if she summoned Bonifacius to Rome,
he would not come.   When the lady heard this, she
approved and followed the advice of Aetius.   The

[1] Professor Freeman, in the English Historical Review for July, 1887.

latter, however, had previously written secretly to Bonifacius that the Emperor's mother was laying snares for his destruction, and as a token of the truth of his assertion he told him that he would find himself without cause suddenly recalled. Hearkening to this warning of Aetius but keeping a profound silence concerning it, when the messengers arrived to invite him to the Imperial Court he declared that he would not obey the Emperor or his mother either. Placidia, on the receipt of this news, looked upon Aetius as a most faithful servant of the throne, but regarded Bonifacius with suspicion. The latter, feeling himself unable to cope with the power of the Emperor, yet accounting himself a doomed man if he started for Rome, began to consider how he could attach the Vandals to his cause, who had obtained possession of the neighbouring province of Spain. Bonifacius, then, having sent to Spain certain of the most influential of his friends, concluded a treaty on terms of equality with both the sons of Godigisclus, to the effect that each of them should receive a third part of Africa, and that if any one of the three were attacked in war, his danger should be shared by the other two.'

So far Procopius. It will be seen that he makes Bonifacius send his invitation to both Kings of the Vandals, but if this were so, certainly before the departure of the host from Spain, Gunderic was dead and Gaiseric was sole ruler of his nation. While he was engaged in his preparations for departure, the King of the Suevi made a devastating

War between Vandals and Suevi.

427.

428.

*Number-
ing of the
people.*

*The Van-
dals trans-
ported to
Africa.*

inroad on the northern part of the Vandal possessions. To show that he was not yet to be thus
contumeliously ignored even on Spanish territory,
Gaiseric suspended his African projects for a while,
turned round and inflicted on the Suevi a bloody
defeat, after which their king was drowned in the
waters of the Gaudiana. Then resuming his plans for
the descent upon Africa, he collected his people
(or rather his two peoples, for he was now always
saluted as King of the Vandals and Alans) upon the
sunny Andalusian shore. Here in the month of
May, 428[1], he had his nation-army numbered, and
found all the males, including old men and little
children, to amount to 80,000. Another computation,
which it is difficult to reconcile with this unless the
limits of age for military service were very wide,
makes the warriors alone amount to 50,000 men.

The ships which Bonifacius, Count of Africa,
supplied from the great port of Carthage, co-operating
with the little fleet of Gaiseric, carried this great
mass of persons, certainly not fewer than 160,000 in
number, to the African coast and landed them,
probably in the province of Numidia. Thus was the
dream of Alaric realised by another German chieftain,
and thus did the intrigues and counter-intrigues of
Roman officials enable a Teutonic invader to strike
at Rome in her most vulnerable point, the great
grain-producing provinces of Africa.

---

[1] The date commonly given is 429, but there are authorities also
for 427 and 428, and upon the whole this last date appears the
most probable.

Scarcely had the Vandals landed on the African
coast when the alliance between them and Bonifacius,
born of treachery and misunderstanding, died in the
daylight of truth.   To resume the narrative of
Procopius.   'All those at Rome who were well acquainted with Bonifacius, reflecting on his character
and the extreme improbability of his being so far
carried away by the desire of reigning, were filled
with wonder at what had taken place. Some of
these persons, by order of Placidia, proceeded to
Carthage, conversed with Bonifacius, saw the letters
of Aetius, and understanding the whole intrigue
returned with all speed to Rome and explained the
position in which Bonifacius had been placed.
Placidia, filled with astonishment, did not dare
openly to blame Aetius, so great was his power and
so necessary his help, in the lamentable state into
which the Empire was falling.   But calling for the
friends of Bonifacius, she explained to them the
secret counsels of Aetius, and binding them to
secrecy by an oath adjured them, if it were possible,
to recall him to the love of his country, and not to
allow the Roman Empire to fall under the yoke of
the barbarians.   When Bonifacius understood all
these things, he was filled with repentance for his
late designs and for the treaty which he had made
with the barbarians, and besought them, with the
lure of many promises, that they would depart from
Africa.   But as the Vandals would not listen to his
words, but rather taunted him with his broken faith
towards them, he was forced to engage in battle with

428.
*Bonifacius
repents of
his treason,
and is re-
conciled to
Placidia.*

Siege of Hippo, June, 430 *to July,* 431. them, and being defeated withdrew to Hippo Regius, a very strong city by the sea-coast of Numidia.

'As the Vandals after a long time could neither take Hippo by storm nor induce it to surrender, and were moreover themselves beginning to suffer from hunger, they broke up the siege. Not long after, Bonifacius and the Romans under his command joined forces with an army sent from Byzantium under the command of Aspar, and dared to try the fortune of war in a great pitched battle, but being much inferior to the enemy, they fled whither they could, and Aspar returned to his own land. But Bonifacius betook himself to the Court of Placidia, and there completely purged himself of the suspicions which had been entertained of him.'

432.

From other sources we learn that Placidia not only forgave Bonifacius but received him into high favour, and conferred upon him the dignity of Master of the Soldiery. Apparently he would have supplanted Aetius in his position of Chief Counsellor of the Empress and virtual ruler of the Empire, but at this moment Aetius returned with his army from a victorious campaign against the Franks, and joined battle with his foe. Aetius was defeated, but Bonifacius lost his life, according to one account, in single combat with his rival, and, strange to say, in the act of dying, adjured his wife to re-marry with Aetius if the death of *his* wife should make such wedlock possible, as he and no other of living Romans was worthy to be the successor as he had been the conqueror of Bonifacius.

The whole story of the rivalry of these two *Strange character of this story.*
Imperial generals is strange, romantic, almost self-
contradictory.　Contemporary annalists scarcely men-
tion it ; later historians tell us a good deal which
it is hardly possible that they could have known.
We should be disposed to send it back into the
region of romance, to which it seems properly to
belong, but for this one clear and all-important fact
—that the Roman governor of Africa did himself
promote' the passage of the Vandals into his province, and only when it was too late and the irre-
trievable mischief was done, turned against them,
and by vain threats and vainer promises, sought to
persuade them to leave the fruitful land into which
he had given them entrance.

Thus, then, at length were the dwellers by the *Result of the Vandal migrations*
Elbe and the Oder settled on the southern shore of
the Mediterranean.　In 406 they were in Pannonia,
in 439 in Carthage.　Thirty-three years, the ordinary
length of a generation, had brought them from
Austria to Tunis, and in their way they had ravaged
Languedoc and set up a short-lived kingdom in
Andalusia.　Remembering always that it was not
a mere army, but a nation, which thus roamed over
mountains and rivers and changed its place of abode
from continent to continent, we feel that the period
of history of which we are now treating is indeed
well named by the Germans *Völker-wanderung,*
'the migration of the nations.'

*Death of
St. Augus-
tine during
the siege
of Hippo,
28 Aug.
430.*
The siege of Hippo Regius (Bona), which has been already alluded to by Procopius, lasted for a little more than thirteen months (June 430 to July 431), and was, as has been already said, one of the few failures of the Vandals. It was memorable in the history of the Church, because the Bishop of Hippo—the greatest of all the bishops of the African Church—St. Augustine, was present within the city at its commencement, and died in the third month of the blockade. His biographer, Possidius, Bishop of Calama, was with him at the end; and from his hand we have an interesting picture of the venerable old man's last days, sitting, as he did, surrounded by bishops from the whole province of Africa, who had seen their cities burned, their churches levelled with the ground, the fruit-trees of the agriculturists torn up by the roots. It was the fury of this first *'Vandal-ism.'* onslaught, and the especial delight taken by the heretical barbarians in the destruction of churches, which caused their name to become a synonym for the demolishers of beautiful buildings. Practically, when we speak of Vandalism, we now generally think of some brutal outrage perpetrated on a temple or a statue; and this in the fifth century would be more probably the work of fanatic monk than of Vandal barbarian. But the deeds of the followers of Gaiseric during the first fury of their conquest, and afterwards, were sufficiently brutal to excuse the opprobrium which the usage of fourteen centuries has linked indissolubly with their name.

After seven years of desolating warfare, peace was

concluded between Gaiseric and the Empire. Aetius *Temporary*
no doubt recognised that the fatal work of Boni- *peace with*
the Em-
facius could not be undone, nor the 50,000 Vandal *pire,* 11
and Alan warriors (reinforced probably by many *Feb.* 435.
Moorish nomads and ruined Roman Provincials)
be forced to relinquish their prey. On his part
Gaiseric had had enough of plundering; he wished
now to occupy and to rule, and he meant to make
the Romans pay a costly price for the peace which
he was willing to concede to them. The strong
city of Hippo, which he had failed to conquer by
force of arms, became his as the result of negotiation.
He had Numidia and the larger part of the African
territory secured to him as his lawful possession,
perhaps on the promised payment of a yearly
tribute[1] to the Emperor, and he had to promise
to leave unmolested Carthage, the capital of the
Roman Diocese and that part of the Province which
immediately adjoined it, a rich and fertile district
certainly, and the gem of the whole dominion.
His son Huneric was sent to Rome as a hostage for
the fulfilment of this condition.

The peace seemed like a confession of something *Gaiseric*
like failure on the part of the Vandal conqueror. *pounces on*
Carthage,
But he had only ' recoiled in order to make a bolder 19 *Oct.*
spring.' He waited his time ; on some pretence or 439.
other he obtained the return of his hostage-son, and
then, while Aetius was busy warring with the Visigoths in Gaul, and Attila from his Hungarian
village was beginning to worry Placidia with his

---

[1] Procopius asserts this.

439.   embassies and his armaments, suddenly, on the 19th
of October, 439, Gaiseric entered Carthage and
made all the vast wealth of the African capital his
own.   Torture was freely used to compel some
of the citizens to yield up to him their hidden
stores.

Appear-   The Vandal king had now reached, apparently,
ance and
character of the summit of his ambition.   Lord of the Roman
Gaiseric. Provinces of Africa and of the great city of Carthage,
he felt himself indeed a king ; and whatever title he
may have borne before, he dated his reign—a reign
which lasted thirty-seven years—from this conquest.
Like Ataulfus, like Attila (one might add, like
Napoleon and like Wellington), he was somewhat
under the usual size, and he had a limp in his gait
owing to a fall from his horse.   He was, by the con-
senting testimony of all contemporary historians, a
man of great ability, admirably preparing his means
to compass the desired ends, simple in his habits, of
few words, patient, and tenacious of purpose ; but on
the other hand, sullen in his wrath, covetous, always
stirring up strife and vexing the nations, and
absolutely ruthless towards all who crossed his
path [1].   In Alaric, notwithstanding some outbursts of
barbaric rage, there was much that was chivalrous
and noble.   Even the dark soul of Attila was ir-
radiated with fitful gleams of generosity and compassion.   But in Gaiseric I do not think we can discern
a single lineament of nobleness.   All is hard, cruel,
vulgar in his remorseless soul.   Alas that we must

[1] This character is chiefly taken from Jordanes, cap. 33.

add, all is also successful in his life. This cruel and
greedy, but supremely able barbarian succeeded
where the nobler Alaric and the gentler Ataulfus
had failed.

His magnificent power of adapting means to ends *His mari-*
was well displayed in the change which he made in *time power*
the habits of his nation after he had become master *tical expe-*
of Carthage. The Vandals, who had dwelt so long on *ditions.*
the skirts of the Riesengebirge, in the highlands
of Austria, or in the plains of Hungary, were essentially an inland people, who only dabbled a little in
seamanship, when they reached the Andalusian
shore. But now that the fleets, the arsenal, the
docks of Carthage were all their own, now that
its harbour—one of the finest in the Old World—
reflected everywhere the Vandal flag, they became
under Gaiseric's guidance the first naval power on
the Mediterranean, and he, by a singular anticipa-
tion of the history of the Barbary States in later
days, made himself the great Buccaneer-King.
With every returning spring his long ships of war
were made ready in the harbour. Sometimes he
ravaged Sicily, sometimes the southern coasts of
Italy, leading the inhabitants of one city into captivity, throwing down the walls of another, wasting
the whole country with his wide-reaching raids. Then
when the very poverty of these lands frighted him
away from their devastated shores, he turned to the
Eastern Empire. Illyricum, Peloponnesus, the islands
of the Ionian and Aegean seas, all that bore the name
of Hellas, bewailed the visits of Gaiseric. Then to

Italy and Sicily again, to try if there were any nook which had hitherto escaped his visitations. At length the work became almost monotonous, and the choice of a victim hard. Once when the fleet had weighed anchor and was sailing forth from the broad harbour of Carthage, the helmsman turned to the king and asked for what port he should steer. 'For the men with whom God is angry,' answered the Vandal king, and left the winds and the waters to settle the question who were the proper objects of the wrath of Heaven.

Vandal land-settle-ment.

The land-settlement of the Vandals and the order of succession to the Vandal throne were two subjects to which Gaiseric's legislative energies were especially directed. (1) The rich Province in which Carthage was situated, called Zeugitana, or the Proconsular Province, the last of all the acquisitions of the Vandals, was portioned out among the warriors of the nation, who received these estates as an inheritance to be transmitted to their children, and who paid no taxes of any kind for them. In the other Provinces, far larger in extent but not nearly so fertile in quality, lay the vast domains of Gaiseric and his sons, consisting of estates forcibly taken away from their Roman owners, often men of culture and noble birth, who were in some cases compelled to cultivate as slaves the lands of which the invader had despoiled them. The poor and barren lands were for the most part left to their former owners, but so burdened with taxes and obligations of service that the unhappy possessors could barely make a livelihood out of them. 'Many of these unhappy possessors tried to flee, but were arrested and executed, sundry grievous charges being brought against them, especially the one unforgivable sin of concealing treasure from Gaiseric. 'Thus,' as the historian[1] says, 'did the Provincials of Africa fall into every kind of misery.'

(2) As for the succession to the throne, in order to avert the rivalries and civil wars which often resulted from the elective character of Teutonic royalty, and at the same time to prevent the crown from being worn by a fatuous boy like Honorius or Valentinian, he ordained that the oldest living male among his descendants should, on the death of each reigning monarch, ascend the Vandal throne. The law was like that which has regulated the succession of the Ottoman Sultans and the Egyptian Pashas. It worked smoothly for near sixty years after the death of Gaiseric, who was succeeded by his eldest son Huneric, he by his two nephews, Gunthamund and Thrasamund, and the latter of these by his cousin Hilderic, the son of Huneric. Then dissensions broke out: Hilderic was dethroned and finally put to death by his cousin Gelimer, but religious differences—for Gelimer was an Arian and Hilderic a Catholic—were the chief cause of these disputes, for which I am not sure that we can fairly blame the Vandal law of succession. *Law of succession to the throne.*

In this allusion to religious differences I have touched upon that which was the distinguishing and *Persecution of the Catholics.*

[1] Procopius.

the shameful characteristic of the Vandal kingdom, especially under Gaiseric and his son ; I mean, their brutal persecution of the Catholics. In their profession of Arianism the Vandals, as we have seen, only followed the example of all the other barbarian nations who had embraced Christianity in any form. Naturally Attila, who worshipped a naked sword, while hating all priests and coveting their costly Communion-plate, was under no temptation to treat the orthodox believers in the Homoousion worse than the Arian believers in the Homoiousion (if any such there yet remained), but would slay both with ferocious impartiality. Naturally, too, the still heathen ancestors of Clovis robbed and murdered the Catholic bishops of Belgic Gaul simply as rich and civilised men, without any special antipathy to them on account of their Catholicism. With the Visigoths, Suevi, and Burgundians the case was different. They were parties to the long Arian lawsuit, and were disposed to depress, and sometimes to harass, the Athanasian litigants on the other side, but they did not systematically persecute, and there are few if any instances of Catholics actually put to death by them for their faith.

Gaiseric, however, seems to have hugged his Arian belief with the fanatical love of a convert, and to have hated the Nicene Confession with the bitter hatred of an apostate. It was indeed reported [1] in

---

[1] Idatius mentions this report: 'Gaisericus qui, ut aliquorum relatio habet, effectus apostata de fide Catholicâ, in Arianam dictus est transisse perfidiam.'

Spain that such was the very truth, that he had
been once a Catholic and had 'apostatised to the
Arian infidelity': but it is difficult to understand
how the son of King Godigisclus can have been
brought up in the Athanasian faith, unless his
illegitimate birth permitted him to be trained by
his mother, probably a Gaulish concubine of the
king, in the despised faith of the Roman Provincials.

Whatever the cause there can be no doubt that
Gaiseric detested the Catholic faith, the faith of the
vast majority of his new subjects, and showed that
detestation by acts of savage cruelty. The churches
were not merely plundered—that the barbarian
hunger for gold would sufficiently account for—but
wantonly burned: and insult was sometimes added
to rapine, as when the beautiful altar-cloths were cut
up and made into shirts and drawers for the grooms of
a barbarian officer. In the regions which paid tribute
to the Palace the bishops were accused of stirring
up the people to revolt, and of likening the king to
Pharaoh, Holofernes, and Nebuchadnezzar: and a
number of them were sent into exile. The Bishop of
Carthage, with several of his clergy, was sent to sea
in a crazy ship, which it was hoped would founder on
the voyage, but arrived safe but penniless on the
shores of Campania. The Metropolitan Church of
Carthage was forbidden to elect any successor to the
exile, and seems to have remained for twenty years
or more 'widowed of its bishop.' The same measure
was meted out to a great number of African Churches,

evidently with the intention of breaking down their episcopal organisation for ever.

In his own palace Gaiseric seemed as if he could not endure the presence of an adherent of the rival creed. Sebastian, the son-in-law of Bonifacius, though a man who was on other grounds acceptable at Court and influential with the king, was put to death because he refused to change his religion. Count Armogast, for the same refusal, was stretched upon the rack, hung head downwards from the ceiling by one foot, and at last sent to do the work of a ditcher and a shepherd in the fields, where he soon died of his hardships.

These and many similar stories which are told us by Victor Vitensis, show the intense and bitter animosity of the great Vandal against all who refused to accept what the ecclesiastical historians call 'the Arian infidelity.' At the same time they fail to bring before us any well-concerted and systematic scheme of persecution, which could by possibility have rooted out the Catholic faith from Africa. Gaiseric was evidently no Diocletian, with sad thoroughness undertaking to eradicate a hostile faith in order to fulfil his duty to the State. Nor was he a Louis XIV, organising dragonnades and revoking edicts of toleration in order that he might keep his mistresses and yet save his soul. He was essentially a barbarian, though a clever one, with all that intolerance of opposition which is shown not by barbarians only when

'Dressed in a little brief authority.'

He could not bear that any of those about him should

dare to belong to any other than 'the King's religion,'
and he tortured, degraded, banished, at last sometimes even killed, in order to punish those who
differed from him for their independence.

Such was the character and such the past career
of the founder of the great Buccaneer State. We
have now to glance at the course of events which, in
the year 455, brought him across the sea to Rome.

Valentinian III, in the year 437, when he had *Family re-*
reached the age of eighteen, went on a visit of state *lations of*
to his cousin, Theodosius II, at Constantinople, and *nian III.*
returned bringing with him that cousin's daughter as
a bride. She bore the name which, with slight
modifications, had been borne by two previous
generations of Imperial ladies in the palace at Constantinople, Eudoxia or Eudocia. Of this marriage
there was no male issue, but two daughters were
born to the Imperial pair, Eudoxia and Placidia.

On the death of Attila (453) the thought, the base *His*
thought, began to insinuate itself into the mind of *jealousy of*
Valentinian that he had now less need of the services *Aetius.*
of the great minister, Aetius. Men called that
minister 'the great safeguard of the Western
Commonwealth and the terror of Attila[1].' His
praises were sung with wearisome repetition, and
the very presence of the strenuous, care-worn warrior
was an oppression and a rebuke to the frivolous
Emperor who 'reigned but did not govern.' The
growing dislike, now that the wise Placidia was laid
in the grave, could be fostered at their pleasure by

[1] Marcellinus Comes, s. a. 454.

454.   the mischief-making lacqueys of the palace, and one
of these, the eunuch Heraclius, for ever seeming to
anticipate the Emperor's wishes, and really making
him the tool of his own base designs, had begun to
talk of possible means of freeing Valentinian from
the yoke of his minister and making him master in
his own house.   Hints of treachery reached the ears
of Aetius, and to secure himself he pressed the
Emperor to exchange with him solemn oaths of
mutual faith.   At the same time a scheme which had
probably been for some time talked of, and which
seemed to promise the undisturbed succession to the
throne of a hero's son, received its final ratification.
Valentinian promised to give one of his daughters in
marriage to Gaudentius [1], the son of Aetius.

Valentini-   Such was the state of affairs, a hollow crust of
an murders reconciliation and plighted vows over the red-hot
Aetius.   lava of hatred and suspicion, when one day Aetius
entered the palace and had an interview with the
Emperor.   He spoke of the covenant entered into
between them : he perhaps urged the completion of
the marriage at once, and hinted that his master was
seeking to evade the fulfilment of his promise.
Valentinian was, or feigned to be, enraged against
his importunate petitioner.   He struck Aetius a
blow : the swords of the surrounding courtiers, we
are told, 'cruelly finished the work.'   The last of the
Romans was lying dead at the feet of one of the
meanest of the Caesars.   Along with Aetius fell one
of his friends, bearer of a name destined to European

          [1] Or possibly Carpilio.   We are not quite sure of the name.

celebrity,—Boetius, an ancestor of the author of the
'Consolation of Philosophy.'

Soon after the foul deed had been done Valentinian
asked a Roman nobleman if he had done well in
slaying Aetius. 'Well done, or ill done, most noble
Augustus, I am hardly able to decide. But I know
one thing, that you have chopped off your right hand
with your left.'

The death of Aetius, which probably occurred *Vengeance*
towards the end of 454, remained not long unavenged. *on Valen-*
Valentinian, who with all his many vices does not *tinian.*
appear to have been a coward, allowed the friends
and retainers of the murdered man to approach him
without hindrance. He supposed that what his
flatterers told him was true, and that the deed of the
Emperor of Rome would be accepted as if it were
the decree of heaven by his adoring subjects. Little
did he know the longing for revenge which filled the
hearts of the barbarian guardsmen of Aetius, who,
like the *Comitatus* of a German chief, deemed themselves for ever disgraced by the unrequited murder
of their lord. On the 16th of March, 455, Valentinian
rode forth from the City to a place called 'the Two
Laurels,' to watch some contest (perhaps a wrestling
match) which was going forward. While he was
intent on the spectacle two henchmen of Aetius,
named Optila and Thraustila [1]—their names reveal
their barbarian origin—approached and 'stabbed
him with unexpected blows [2].' The eunuch He-

[1] Or Accila and Trasila (Continuator Prosperi). Trasila is here
said to have been a son-in-law of Aetius.

[2] 'Insperatis et inopinatis ictibus confoderunt.'

raclius, who had been his accomplice in the murder
of Aetius, was slain at the same time.

*Accession
of Maxi-
mus.*

With the death of Valentinian the dynasty of
Theodosius came to an end, his cousin Pulcheria,
the Augusta at Constantinople, having died two years
before (453). The person who was chosen to succeed
him was Maximus, an elderly Senator, a man who had
been twice Consul, and had filled various offices of
the State with credit and distinction. The hopes
which had been formed of a wise and honourable
administration of the affairs of the Republic by the
new Emperor were, however, soon disappointed.
Maximus not only left the murder of his predecessor
unavenged : he even seemed ostentatiously to court
the society of the murderers, thus definitely enrolling
himself as a partisan of the family of Aetius and an
antagonist of the probably still numerous adherents
of the Theodosian house. He carried this partisanship to such lengths as to suggest to the minds of
his subjects that he had himself been privy to the
death of his predecessor. The suspicion was
probably unfounded, but the mere fact that it was
widely entertained must have been fatal to the moral
ascendency of the new Emperor. Moreover he com-

*His mar-
riage with
·Eudoxia.*

pelled the beautiful widow of Valentinian, who was
still truly mourning her unworthy husband, to accept
his hand in marriage, and proposed to marry his son
Palladius to her daughter, Placidia. If he hoped
thus to consolidate his dynasty by a double union
with the family of his predecessor, he was bitterly disappointed. Eudoxia was wounded in her affections

by the indecent haste with which she had been com- *455.* pelled to accept this elderly and commonplace civil servant instead of the brilliant, if worthless, husband of her youth. She was wounded in her pride by a marriage, or rather by two marriages, deemed by her to be beneath the dignity of that great Theodosian house to which she belonged by a double title, and which had now for three quarters of a century been, in the flattering dialect of the Court, 'domus divina.'

Like her sister-in-law Honoria, in her rage and *Eudoxia* despair she looked to the barbarian for aid. She *invokes the* found means to send a messenger to Gaiseric, in- *aid of Gai-* viting him to attack Rome and deliver her from *seric.* shameful bondage. The messenger found the Vandal king in no unwilling mood. Most likely he had often discussed with himself the probabilities of success or failure in the most brilliant enterprise that ambition and avarice could suggest to a Teutonic warrior : and now all doubts were removed by the knowledge that Rome's powers of resistance, feeble at the best, would be paralysed by internal dissensions. His ships were no doubt all equipped in readiness for his usual spring-tour of desolation : he had but to give to the waiting pilot the word of command, 'for Rome.'

The Vandal fleet reached the mouth of the Tiber *Gaiseric* in the early days of June (455) ; but already, three *sets sail for* days before their arrival, the reign of Maximus, *Rome,* which lasted only about ten or eleven weeks, had *June, 455.* come to an end. The rumour of the impending invasion, fears of domestic treachery, the unconcealed

455. scorn and hatred of Eudoxia, quite unnerved the elderly Emperor, who, after publishing a proclamation granting liberty to leave the City to all who desired to do so, himself claimed the permission which he had accorded to his subjects and stole away from the palace. As soon as his departure was discovered an insurrection broke out. The servants of the palace, who were all on Eudoxia's side, followed and

Flight and death of Maximus. overtook the fugitive. According to the ghastly precedent set in the case of Rufinus, they tore him limb from limb, dragged the pieces of his body through the streets of Rome and hurled them contemptuously into the Tiber. Already, in the general ruin of society, the men who called themselves Romans were showing themselves even more barbarous than the barbarians.

Surrender of the City. A city thus left without a ruler, and probably divided against itself, (the enemies and the friends of the late Theodosian dynasty regarding one another with hatred and fear,) could offer no effectual resistance, and appears to have offered no resistance at all, to the mighty Vandal. Once more the expedient of Papal intercession was resorted to, but this time with only partial success. When Pope Leo with his clergy met Gaiseric outside the Porta Portuensis the conqueror agreed—no doubt on condition that his entry should be unopposed—to spare the lives of the inhabitants, to set fire neither to church, palace, nor private dwelling, and to abstain from the use of torture for the discovery of hidden wealth. These conditions being observed, there was to be no limit to the Vandal capacities for spoliation. 'For four- teen days,' says an annalist[1], 'with secure and unhindered investigation, Rome was stripped of all her wealth.' Temple and Christian church were impartially plundered. Half of the gilded roof of the Temple of Capitolian Jove, the Communion-plate of all the great basilicas, statues from forum and hippodrome and villa, the crown and jewelled ornaments of Theodosius and his posterity, even the seven-branched candlestick and the table of the shew-bread which Titus had brought from ruined Jerusalem, these and endless other treasures were borne during those fourteen days of leisurely spolia-tion along the Via Portuensis and stowed away in the capacious holds of the Vandal galleys[2]. The vessel which bore the statues and other treasures of art most unfortunately foundered on the voyage. The spoils of the Jewish temple reached their destination in safety, and after reposing in the recesses of the Vandal palace at Carthage for seventy-nine years were carried to Constantinople to grace the triumph of Belisarius: but the Roman Emperor Justinian, fearing that these sacred treasures which had already witnessed the sack of three great cities, Jerusalem,

455.
*Plunder
of Rome.*

---

[1] Prosper.

[2] We are not distinctly told that the fleet of Gaiseric lay at anchor off Portus, but this is rather more probable than that they were at Ostia. It is quite possible, however, that the fleet may have been divided between the two ports when it was plain that there was to be no opposition. This would enable the Vandals to load much more cargo during the fourteen days, which on any hypothesis seems rather a short time for the immense amount of business transacted in them.

455.

Rome, and Carthage, bringing ill fortune with them like the Ark of God to the cities of the Philistines, might also witness the fall of Constantinople, sent them back to their original home on Mount Moriah, where apparently they must still have been stored up when Omar, at the head of his true believers, stormed the Holy City.

Gaiseric returns to Africa.

Gaiseric, having fully accomplished his purpose, not conquest but plunder, returned to Carthage, laying waste on his way the shores of Campania and ruining the cities of Capua and Nola. The Empress Eudoxia and her two daughters were transported to Carthage. The elder daughter, Eudoxia, was married to Gaiseric's eldest son, Huneric,—a most miserable union, since she was a devoted Catholic and her husband a bitter Arian. In 472, after twenty-seven years of wedlock, she escaped from the hated land to Jerusalem, and there died, after a few months spent in religious seclusion, at the Tomb of the Saviour. The Empress Eudoxia and her other daughter, Placidia, were sent to Constantinople in 462, after seven years' captivity, in consideration of a large ransom paid by the Emperor Leo, who, though no relation of the Theodosian family, felt his dignity wounded by the detention of the widow and daughter of an Emperor in the palace of the barbarian.

Captivity of Eudoxia and her daughters.

Further fortunes of the Theodosian family.

Placidia's husband, a senator named Olybrius, was one of the 'shadow-Emperors' whose coming and going marked the last twenty years of the Empire of the West. In March, 472, he was proclaimed Augustus by Ricimer, the successor of Stilicho and

Aetius in the position of 'powerful friend' of the
Emperors. In October of the same year he died of
dropsy, having produced no perceptible eddy in the
swift downward current of the fortunes of Rome.
A grandson of his and Placidia's, a great-grandson
of Valentinian III, named also Olybrius, was Consul
in 491. His inconspicuous name is the last vestige
left in history of the family of the great Theodosius.

I have overpassed the proper limits of my subject
by a few years in order to trace the fortunes of the
Theodosian *family*. The Theodosian *dynasty* ended,
as we have seen, in March, 455; and that event,
with the immediately succeeding sack of Rome by
Gaiseric, is a fitting close to my narrative.

In 375, before the Huns had crossed the Dniester, *Conclu-*
or the fugitive Visigoths had crowded to the shore *sion.*
of the Danube, beseeching the hospitality of the Empire, it seemed as if the stately fabric reared by the
Senate and People of Rome, which had already
stood for eleven centuries, might stand for eleven
centuries more. In 455, when the ships of the Vandal king were bearing away the widow and daughters
of an Emperor, the spoils of the city and palace, and
a crowd of well-born captives, to his robber-fortress
of Carthage, the sceptre of the great world-conquering
power was broken. Britain, Gaul, Germany, Spain,
Africa, were lost to her dominion. Rome herself
had twice surrendered to a barbarian conqueror, and
had twice been sacked by his soldiers. The sacred
soil of Italy had for years been trodden under foot

by the armies of the Goth, the Hun, and the Vandal. The Empire's reputation of unconquerableness had departed from her, and when Roman and barbarian met on the battle-field, the expectation in both armies was that the legions would *not* be victorious. A long and wonderful existence yet lay before the New Rome by the Bosphorus, but from the Old Rome by the Tiber the spell of Empire had for a time departed. Yet already there were indications in the sky from what quarter her new day would dawn. Already the majestic figure of Leo betokened the uprising of a new order of men, the avowed successors of a fisherman of Bethsaida, who should rule over a wider world than the Roman Empire, and wield a more absolute authority than had been enjoyed by the proudest of the successors of Augustus.

INDEX.

(Modern place-names in Italics.)

A.

Ad Salices (the Willows), battle of, 94.

Aemona (*Laybach*), 127, 131, 153.

Aequitius, Superintendent of the Palace, 100.

Aetius, 178, 191–210, 225, 226.

Agathias, 40 *n.*, 41 *n.*

Agentes in Rebus, 42.

Alamanni, 25, 74.

Alani, 124, 152, 182, 196, 206.

Alaric, 131, 137–168.

Alatheus the Ostrogoth, 96, 97.

Alavivus, 87, 91.

Ambrose, St., 122.

Ammianus Marcellinus, 45, 47, 49, 102, 124.

Angles, 183.

Anianus, Bishop of Paris, 194.

Antioch, 23, 118–120.

Aquileia—besieged by Attila, 198.

Arbogast, 110, 128–132.

Arcadius, 36 *n.*, 117, 134, 141, 142, 153, 155.

Ardaburius the Alan, 177.

Ardaric, King of the Gepidae, 196.

Arian controversy, 31.

Ariminum, plains of, 164, 172.

Aristocracy of Rome, not theoretically hereditary, 8 ; manners of, in fourth century, 47–48.

Armogast, Count, 224.

Army, Roman, size of, in the fourth century, 39–40.

Ascholius, Bishop of Thessalonica, 109.

Aspar the Alan, 177.

Ataulfus, 172–175, 208.

Athanaric (Judge of the Visigoths), 79, 86, 111, 112.

Attalus, 162–164, 174.

Attila, King of the Huns, 180–203.

Augustine, St., 216.

Augustus, work of, 14.

B.

Bacurius, 131.

Baltic, the, 183, 184.

Barbaricum, 76, 79.

Barritus, the, 94.

Batvin (Gothic martyr), 79.

Bauto, the Frank, 110, 128, 142.

Bleda, King of the Huns, 180.

Bonifacius, Governor of Africa, 179, 209–214.

Bora, a fierce wind, 131.

Botheric, 121.

Bretons, the, 196.

Britain, invasion of by Angles and Saxons, 183–184.

Britain, Roman roads in, 2–4.

Brutus, 12.

Burgundians, the, 180, 196.

Busentus, the, Alaric buried in, 168.

C.

Caesar, work of, 13, 14 ; on the Germans, 55.

Caesarius, 119, 120.

Camps, 20.

Carthage, Vandals at, 215, 218–220.

Cassiodorus, 49.

Castinus, Magister Militum, 177, 209.

Cauca (in Spain, the birthplace of Theodosius), 105.

Celtic nationality, 73.

Censorship, 9.
Châlons, battle of, so called, 195.
China, 183.
Christian legislation of Constantine, 30, 51 n.
Christianity, relation of Diocletian to, 28.
— relation of Constantine to, 29.
— relation of Constantine's successors to, 31.
Chrysopolis, battle of, 27.
Chrysostom, St. John, 120.
Clarissimi, class of, 43.
Claudian, 144.
Clovis and the vase of Soissons, 69 n.
Coinage, Imperial, of 1st and 3rd centuries contrasted, 19.
Coloni, condition of, 51–52.
Comes Privatarum Rerum, 42.
— Sacrarum Largitionum, 42.
Consistory, Imperial, 37.
Constantine the Great, 24, 31, 51 n.
— the Usurper, 152, 163, 207.
Constantinople, foundation of, 26 ; siege of, 101.
Constantius I, 24–25.
— husband of Placidia, 176.
— secretary to Attila, 184, 185.
Crispus, son of Constantine, 27.
Crocus, king of the Alamanni, 25.
Curiales, 52–53.

D.

Dahn, F., 60 n.
Damasus, Pope, 109.
Decurio, 52.
Diocletian, his work of restoration, 21–25 ; his death, 26 ; his relation to Christianity, 28.

E.

East, Prefecture of, 23.
Edeco the Hun, 186.
Ellebichus, 119, 120.
Emperor, Roman, appearance of, 34, 35 ; titles of, 36.

Ernak, son of Attila, 190, 203.
Eucherius, 155, 158.
Eudoxia, wife of Arcadius, 142.
— wife of Valentinian III, 225, 228, 232.
— daughter of Valentinian III, 225 ; married to Huneric, 232.
Eugenius, Emperor, 130, 131.
Eutropius, 142.
Extortion of Roman Governors, 11, 17.

F.

Fiesole, 149.
Firmus, 106.
Flaccilla, 126.
Flavianus, Bishop of Antioch, 118–120.
Food supply of Roman citizens, 48, 49.
Franks, 74, 152, 179, 196.
Freceric (Gothic martyr), 79.
Freeman, E. A., 65 n., 210 n.
Frigidus, battle of, 131.
Fritigern, Visigothic chieftain, 79, 86, 87, 91, 92, 96, 97, 111.

G.

Gainas the Goth, 131, 140, 141.
Gaiseric, King of the Vandals, 192, 209–234.
Galerius, colleague of Diocletian, 24.
Galla, wife of Theodosius, 126, 130.
Galla Placidia (see Placidia).
Games of the circus, 49.
Gau (= pagus), 65.
Gaudentius, father of Aetius, 178.
— son of Aetius, 226.
Gauls, prefecture of the, 22, 23.
Gelimer, King of the Vandals, 221.
Geougen, the, 183.
Gepidae, 182, 195, 202.
Germania of Tacitus, 55.
German kingship, 67–72.
— popular assemblies, 70–72.
Germans, condition of, 54–72.
Gerontius, 207.

Godigisclus, King of the Vandals, 206.
'Gothic Architecture,' 75; Gothic Christianity, 78; Gothic language, 76.
Goths, 75. See Visigoths, Ostrogoths.
Gratian, 91, 95, 105, 110, 111, 123–125.
Greuthungi (= Ostrogoths?), 86 *n.*
Gunderic, King of the Vandals, 208, 209.
Gunthamund, King of the Vandals, 221.

H.

Hadrianople, battle of (323), 27.
— — (378), 96, 100.
Helena, mother of Constantine, 24.
Heraclian, 163, 167.
Heraclius the Eunuch, 226, 228.
Hermanric, King of the Ostrogoths, 76, 85.
Heruli, 182, 195, 202.
Hilderic, King of the Vandals, 221.
Hippo, siege of, 214, 216.
Hispalis (*Seville*) taken by Vandals, 209.
Honoria, 185, 192.
Honorius, 134, 146, 152–157, 161–164, 166, 176.
Huneric, 217.
Huns, 180, 193; description of, by Jordanes, 81, 83; ethnological character of, 84; enter Europe (374), 85.

I.

Ildico, wife of Attila, 202.
Illustres, class of, 37.
Illyricum, Prefecture of, 23.
Ingenuus, 174.
Italy, Prefecture of, 23.

J.

Jerome, St., 45, 47, 174.
Joannes, Emperor, 177.

Jordanes (Gothic historian, wrote cir. 550), 81–83.
Jovian, 90.
Jovius, Praetorian prefect, 161–162.
'Judges' of the Visigoths, 76.
Julian 'the Apostate,' 90.
Julius, master of the soldiery, 104.
Justina, 91, 126, 128.
Jutes, the, 183.

K.

Kingship and national unity, 67.

L.

Lampadius, 153.
Lancearii, 98.
Land—settlement of the Germans, 60–62.
Latifundia, 50, 51.
Leo I, Pope, 200, 230.
Leo, Emperor, 232.
Libanius, 120.
Licinius, his struggle with Constantine, 27.
Lupicinus, Count of Thrace, 88–93.
Lupus, St., Bishop of Troyes, 195, 198.

M.

Magister Militiae, 39–40.
Magister Officiorum, 42.
Marcian, Emperor, 191.
Marcianople (*Shumla*), 92–93.
Marcomanni, 74.
Maria, wife of Honorius, 154.
Mattiarii, 98.
Maxentius, Emperor, 26.
Maximian, Emperor, 24, 26.
Maximin Daza, Emperor, 24.
— ambassador to Attila, 186.
Maximus (a wealthy citizen of Rome), 47.
Maximus, Duke of Moesia, 88–93.
— Magnus Clemens, usurper, 123, 125, 126.

Maximus, Emperor, 207, 228, 229.
Milan (Mediolanum), 23.
Money, purchasing power of, 46 *n.*

N.

Nicaea, Council of, 29–30.
Nicomedia in Bithynia, 24–25.
Nicopolis, city of, owned by Paula, 47.
Notitia Utriusque Imperii, 38, 39, 40 *n.*, 41, 42, 44.

O.

Oath taken by soldiers to Emperor, 36.
Offices, sale of, under the Empire, 43.
Official hierarchy of the Empire, 37–44.
Olybrius, 'Shadow-Emperor,' 232.
Olympius, 155–157, 159.
Onegesius the Hun, 187, 188.
Optila, henchman of Aetius, 227.
Orleans, siege of, 194.
Orosius, 172.
Ostrogoths, 75, 76, 99, 182, 195, 202.

P.

Pagus, German, 65–66.
Paris, 194.
Paula, piety and wealth of, 47.
Persian Empire, relation of, to Roman, 6–7.
Placidia, daughter of Theodosius, 130, 171, 174–180, 184, 191.
Placidia, daughter of Valentinian III, 225, 228, 232.
Pliny, 50.
Pollentia, battle of, 146.
Possidius, Bishop of Calama, 216.
Praefectus Annonae, 49.
— Praetorio, office of, 38, 39.
Praepositus Sacri Cubiculi, 41.
Prefectures, the four great, 22–3.

Priscus, ambassador to Attila, 186, 189.
Probus, wealth of, 46.
Procopius, 166, 210.
Proculus, 136.
Proletariate, 46 *n.*
Pulcheria, sister of Theodosius II, 191, 228.

Q.

Quaestor, 42.

R.

Radagaisus, 145, 146, 148, 149.
Ravenna, Honorius at, 146.
Richomer, Count of the Domestics, 97.
Ricimer, 232.
Roman Empire, boundaries of, 1–7.
Romanus, 106.
Rome, sieges of, 159 ; entered by Alaric, 164 ; plunder of, by the Vandals, 231.
Rufinus, Praetorian Prefect, 135–142.

S.

Salarian Gate, Alaric enters Rome through, 164.
Sallust, palace of, burned, 165.
Sangiban, King of the Alani, 196.
Saphrax, Ostrogothic chief, 96, 97.
Sarmatians, 73, 74.
Sarus the Goth, 149, 157, 164.
Saulus the Alan, 131, 147.
Saxons, the, 183, 196.
Sebastian, General, 96, 100.
— son-in-law of Bonifacius, 224.
Seebohm, F., 62, 58 *n.*
Senate of Rome, 7–9 ; behaviour of Emperors to, 15–16.
Serena, 136, 153, 160.
Severus, 24.
Siege artillery, Roman, 102.
Silentiarii, 33.
Silvanus the Goldsmith, 185.
Singeric, 175.

Sirmium, 23–95.
— vases of, 184, 185, 192.
Slaves, condition of, 50, 51.
Slavonic nationality, 73.
Spalato (near Salona), 27 *n.*
Spectabiles, class of, 38.
Stilicho, 135–158.
Stubbs, Bishop, 65 *n.*
Suevi, 182, 206.
Symmachus, wealth of, 46.

T.

Tacitus, Germania of, 55, 60–62, 68, 71.
Tatianus, 136.
Theodoric, King of the Visigoths, 192–3.
Theodosius the Elder, 106.
— the Great, 105, 106–133, 139.
— II, son of Arcadius, 155, 177, 186, 191.
— son of Ataulfus and Placidia, 175.
Thermantia, wife of Honorius, 154, 158.
Thessalonica, 121, 126.
Thincsus, epithet of German Mars, 70 *n.*
Thing, meeting of the Folk, 70.
Thiudans (= king in Gothic), 72.
Thorismund the Visigoth, 196, 197.
Thrasamund, King of the Vandals, 221.
Thraustila, henchman of Aetius, 227.
Ticinum (*Pavia*), 156.
Trajan, General-in-Chief, 100.
Tribunician power, 10.
Trier (Augusta Trevirorum), 23.

U.

Uldin the Hun, 149.
Ulfilas, Apostle of the Goths, 77, 78, 110.

V.

Valens, Emperor, 87–98.
Valentinian I, 90, 91.
— II, 91, 125–129.
— III, 177, 184, 191, 200, 225–7.
Valerian, Count of Imperial Stables, 100.
Vandals, the, 204–232.
Venice, foundation of, 199.
Victor, son of usurper Maximus, 128.
Victor Vitensis, 224.
Village settlements of the Germans, 57, 58.
Visigoths, 75, 87–99, 179.
Völker-wanderung, the, 215.

W.

Waitz, G., 60 *n.*
Walamir, King of the Ostrogoths, 196.
Walia, King of the Visigoths, 176.
Wealthy Romans, fortunes of, 46.

Y.

York (Eboracum), 25–26.

Z.

Zercon, the Moor, 190.
Zosimus, 133.

THE END.